Ten Hours with
GOD

Dana A. Solla

Ten Hours with GOD

How to Discover Your Gifts and Learn to Walk in Your Calling

TATE PUBLISHING
AND **ENTERPRISES**, LLC

Published by Tate Publishing & Enterprises, LLC
127 E. Trade Center Terrace | Mustang, Oklahoma 73064 USA
1.888.361.9473 | www.tatepublishing.com

Tate Publishing is committed to excellence in the publishing industry. The company reflects the philosophy established by the founders, based on Psalm 68:11,
"The Lord gave the word and great was the company of those who published it."

Book design copyright © 2014 by Tate Publishing, LLC. All rights reserved.
Cover design by Junriel Boquecosa
Interior design by Jomar Ouano

Published in the United States of America
ISBN: 978-1-62854-447-3
1. Religion / General
2. Religion / Christian Life / General
13.11.26

Stop!

Now that you have this book in your hands, don't put it down!

God has given it to you for a purpose. This is your moment in time, the hour of His visitation.

God has a gift for you, claim it! Don't let it go! It is yours...

Another tool of the restoration arsenal.

Ten Hours with God is not just a coffee table devotional book.

Ten Hours with God takes you to a place called Commitment and Change.

If you make this commitment, your Ten Hours will last a life time. Dana makes the connection between God, time, and change. Reading this book is time well spent.

—Pastor Joel Alvarado
Breaking Free Ministry
The Rock Church and World Outreach Center

Dedication

I would like to make a dedication to the Holy Spirit for the revelation of this book and it finally making into print. As I was preparing to write my next book I had in mind a very different work. While at church the Spirit of the Lord revealed to me that this book "Ten Hours with God" was the work that needed to be done. It is more than a book to me, it is a ministry.

There are so many people, of all ages, that really don't know their calling or what their gifting is. Some have searched an entire life time and still don't know. They have spent their whole life doing what was expected of them to provide for their families or they just got caught up paying bills and surviving day to day and month to month with a promise; "one of these days I will look into what I have always wanted to do." It maybe that you need to enroll in a school and take those classes or spend time in the library researching to prepare yourself; Don't be one those who just never found the time to do it. I am here to proclaim to you your search is over, you don't need to search any more. What you have been looking for is already there it is right inside of you. No longer do you need to run and hide or be afraid to do what is in your heart because you weren't sure you could. For some it is what you have always dreamed of, don't give up on your dreams. Pick it up, start doing it and God will provide for you away, the secret you need to know is that it is not outside of you it is inside and always has been.

There are also those who are just starting out in life and have no clue what it is that they want to do with their lives. They question what their calling and gifts are and doubt it all they get caught up with doing the same thing as the generation before did, take a job or career because they need a job. They go for higher education and get degrees in fields that they will never work in. We know these things are true because statistics show us that most people who graduate college are not working in the fields in which they earned their degrees. If it is a 4 year degree it may have taken them 5 or 6 years to earn because of the over crowding for the classes that they need. Then of course is the cost of the education, the student loans that follow for years and years after graduation.

This ministry the Holy Spirit has revealed to me, through the writing of this book, is to reach Gods children and to let them know He loves us and has a plan for our lives. He wants us to seek Him out and have a relationship with Him. He wants us to know He is a loving Father and has a purpose for us in this life. He has gifted each of us with certain talents to accomplish this purpose. We just need to find out what these gifts and talents are and He has provided for us a way to discover what they are. He wants us to use these gifts and be a blessing to others and give Him glory for it. It is our job to discover and polish this gift, it is to become our labor or work, and once we have polished our gift our job becomes sharing it with others.

I believe that God has put greatness in all of us and it is up to us to discover what it is.

The one thing I believe, more than anything else, is that He is wanting a personal relationship with each and every one of use, a daily contact through prayer that lead us through this life making it rewarding and a life worth living. I also believe that when it is all said and done and we go before our maker we also want to hear the words "well done good and faithful servant."

The greatness that has been placed inside of us can be anything it can be becoming president of the United States of America, a four-star general, a multibillionaire, scientist, inventor, writer, or teacher. We can be farmers, doctors, and lawyers; we can be mothers and fathers. We can be anything our heart desires, but most of all we can be what God has called us to be. The greatness is that we are fulfilled in what it is we do and when we are it brings joy and satisfaction a comforting in knowing all the hard work, dedication and faith in God is worth it.

The way to start this great and glorious journey of discovery and fulfillment is to spend "Ten Hours with God" it will give you hope, it will build your faith and give you your hearts desire.

Contents

Foreword

It is not easy staying on a diet or pushing aside our fun things to study school books or the Holy Scriptures; and if you ever had a new year's membership to a health club, it may not have lasted long. Even being a self-starter and a believer in large scale, grand projects, it is wonderfully refreshing to have others encourage and stimulate my earnest efforts. Let's be honest, we all could use a life coach or personal trainer. Author Dana Solla, can be that guide to millions if they will just listen and do the will of the Lord. We all have greatness wired into us, we just need to "relearn" and proclaim the victory. Once you get "it," share it! Even with enemies. Dana's constant upbeat and refreshing enthusiasm makes this guide to the universal truth an easy and fun read, to tune the mind to a deeper focus on the word itself while opening us up to wise and far-reaching truths. Pray, fast, train, plant, nurture, live, love, harvest, hope, trust, and accept.

Author Dana Solla's manuscript is not a laminated "cheat sheet" to get you past the spiritual enlightenment test nor your involvement in it; you must still participate, so put in the time and energy to stretch and retrain your mind toward the will of God. If you follow through with the program, you will be blessed.

Do you have vision? If your first thought was the ability to see, then you are probably lacking in the area of future vision and personal dream fulfillment. This book will be the key to attaining or reinvigorating that purpose and more in your life.

As a devout nonfiction reader, Dana's first effort, *Christians' House*, brought me back to the fiction fold with his mixture of facts within the novel. This latest foray into the psyche of the reader pulls no punches, which is right up my alley. Straightforward, positive, and useful information and strategies for implementation—those are why I highly recommend *Ten Hours with God*, his latest masterpiece.

Mr. Solla's great-granduncle was the late and wonderfully colorful Samuel Clemens, aka Mark Twain. He tends to shy away from comparisons as they are enormous shoes to fill. I foresee Mr. Solla, provided the Lord allows us his extended company, developing into one of the foremost spiritual writers of our time. *Ten Hours with God* reminded me of C.S. Lewis's *The Screw Tape Letters*, Dana jumps right in the battle but with the care and gentleness befitting a child of God. Perhaps it is derived from his brief days on the professional ball field where injury cut short his career of promise but soon developed a caring heart for others with injuries and for their personal challenges. After reading his books, I'm sure you will agree and make them your Christmas stocking stuffers.

More important than keeping our immune system healthy is the strengthening of our spiritual well-being through much training and exercise. Once your spiritual will weakens, the end begins, unless you turn your inner compass around. Give this book your full attention—to the point of reading it several times. Read *Ten Hours with God* three times; the first time, you will know there is something to be attained; second time, to participate with intent to follow the instructions; and third, polish what God has given you and implement. Remember that in the wild of the natural world and that of the spirit, the strongest beast and predators, such as lions, tigers, and demons, always go after the weakest link in the herd; they smell the blood, feel the fear, and crave the power of death. They start to become less timid and get *bolder* as each moment passes. Please do not be that weak link! Put on the full armor of God.

You will be asked to do several things in this relationship including getting three green strands, braiding them together, and tying them around your wrist to represent bond and strength. As I sat down to read the original manuscript, I thought Dana was really trying to make this difficult. Nevertheless, I understand the importance of faith and action, so the three green strands I braided were quickly torn from my walking shorts. It reminded me of the General who was looking for a miracle and was told to dip three times in the Jordan River; he became angry and stated that his own rivers were cleaner. Who am I? Who are you? Just get in the water and dip. It does not matter if your river is cleaner or not, just do it!

You will be asked to do other things like fast during your chapter reading, please don't over think these, just do them and believe.

Sitting down with a bowl of trail mix to begin chapter 2, the "fasting" chapter, and forgetting the criteria set forth by the author, I quickly gobbled down the mix followed by a cup of coffee and dove in. Later, while in the middle of the chapter, I was called in for dinner. I've come to believe that honoring my wife by eating her food at dinner time is a good way to keep our marriage healthy. To add insult to injury, I then followed with a delicious smelling yogurt facial which stayed on the duration of the chapter! How ironic, during the "fasting" chapter, I could not have had more food in or on me, yet I would not give up with self-condemnation or ridicule as the enemy would have me! We must carry on, which I did!

Fortunately, we have a very kind and loving God, loving enough to give us Jesus Christ on the cross and even look through our silliness. Please observe the fasting rule as it is helpful and remember, a fast can be anything (food or other) that denies the flesh for a predetermined period of time and for a purpose (Faith, Overcoming, Restoration).

From chapter one, which I call "pray, pray, pray," to chapter 10, appropriately titled "God Restores," author Dana Solla brings out the full artillery of God and uses an incredible ability to change gears as illustrated from his first breakout novel *Christians' House*—a must-read tome, which is really a type of quick guide or reference to the larger manual, in this case, the Holy Scriptures.

So spend an hour with God each day, after all, He set aside a whole day for you. Go to church to dwell upon the Lord, Yahweh, and He will dwell within you. Spend time with God, not only for yourself but do it for family, friends, neighbors, and others so that God may be honored through His blessings in you, and remember, "The misery that you go through is the ministry that you are called to." Expect miracles, after all, it is your faith and no one else's.

Use this book to become addicted to God through prayer and scriptural study.

Best regards and love in Christ Jesus,
—Sir Kenneth Lee Beaver

Preface

The writing of *Ten Hours with God* came as nothing but pure inspiration and a purpose.

I was sitting in church with my wife on a beautiful Sunday morning; it was during first service at eight a.m. We like to go to the early service.

There was a guest speaker this particular morning, and to say he was quite dynamic would be an understatement. To say he was full of the Holy Spirit and delivering a message that had your full attention would be more accurate.

In the middle of his message, he seemed to lose his train of thought. For an instant his concentration was broken, as if someone else was speaking to him and he was trying to hold two conversations simultaneously.

A moment later, he gathered himself and went right back into his message, having picked up exactly where he left off.

It really wasn't all that noticeable at the time; but very shortly afterward, he did it again. This time it was very noticeable.

He stopped and said, "Okay, Lord! I will!"

As he said this, he stepped away from the pulpit, his eyes looked up and down and then across the entire auditorium as if he was searching for someone in particular. There was a somewhat bewildered look on his face as he walked slowly across the platform.

Looking around at the congregation, he continued.

"I apologize, but when you are preaching the word of God and you are being led by the Holy Spirit, you must obey what it is that He is saying to you, even if it comes in the middle of your message." He rolled his eyes and shrugged his shoulders.

"Even if it is something that you did not plan on saying, you must be obedient to His call. So that's why I stopped when I did, the Holy Spirit is telling me to do something right now; and I don't know why, but I feel I must do what He is telling me to do. Maybe this is for someone in here I don't know, but I am obligated to do as God is instructing me."

Everybody in the place was a little shocked at all this; after all, this is not the typical behavior of a guest speaker. People were wondering what it was that he was doing. The senior pastor even had a what-is-going-on-here look; both he and his wife looked at each other with a curious and bemused look as everybody glanced over to them to get some kind of signal as to whether this was a planned thing or not. But you could tell just by looking at them that they were just as surprised as everybody else.

This guest speaker certainly had every one's attention at this point. He walked over to where the senior pastors sat, gestured again with his hands and shrugged shoulders, and went on. "The Holy Spirit said to me that there is someone in here that is a writer." Again, he paused for just an instant and then said "no! I don't understand" as he hesitated and scratched his clean-shaven chin. He lifted his hands with outstretched arms to God. He was a big man—maybe six foot three or six foot four, two hundred fifty pounds, late forties or early fifties—he carried himself with a certain confidence, his countenance was strong and secure, and you know that the Spirit of God was in him.

He continued, "Let me ask this, is anyone here a writer or an author, someone who writes books like novels or something?"

With that, my wife elbowed me in the side—all you married men know exactly what I am talking about. He said, "Raise up your hand."

I had just started in my walk as an author that year and was still somewhat hesitant on declaring it publicly, even though I had a couple of articles published. I had finished writing my first novel and had signed a contract with a traditional publisher. It was still in the editing process at the time and not yet out at the bookstores. So technically, I did qualify as an author.

At my wife's ever-so-subtle encouragement, I raised my right hand up into the air with a small degree of discomfort, though not so much from the public acknowledgement as an author.

There were maybe three other people who raised their hands as well.

Our church sits somewhere in the area of about three thousand plus people, so there really weren't many people considering the total number that lives there.

The guest speaker was no more than ten feet away from me at that time, as he had moved to our side of the platform when he first stepped away from the pulpit.

He went on to say, "One of you needs to come see me after service; I have a message for you."

He then turned right back around, went to the pulpit, and started preaching again saying, "Sometimes you just need to stop what you are doing, and do what it is that the Holy Spirit is directing you to do."

He said, "When we as preachers tell you how to follow what it is God says do, we need also be alert enough to recognize when God is speaking to us and act upon it."

Then he went back into his message and hadn't lost a beat. When he finished with his message, the church had its altar call and was emptying out; he stood up near the front of the platform, just below the pulpit.

I waited for a moment to see if anyone else approached him from what he had said earlier.

My wife asked me, "Are you going to go up to him?"

I said, "I don't know, maybe somebody else will."

"You should go speak with him; maybe it is a calling for you. But you won't know if you don't do what God said do. Are you an author or not?"

"Yes, I am and I declare it. I acknowledge it, and I walk in it. I am an author, and I do write novels and books."

You see, I was trying to talk myself into believing what it was that I believe God has called me to do and be true to it. Sometimes, it takes courage to step into something that you have always dreamt of and at the same time have doubts, thoughts, and fears of ridicule and failure. It's funny; sometimes, we don't do what we are called to do because of the fear of failure or the unfamiliar ground of success. So sometimes, people who are afraid of rejection go into professions like sales, or become stand-up comedians, or perhaps even preachers and end up dealing with the fear of rejection all of their lives. It is that very thing that draws them to what they do. Some may argue: "what is the difference between a salesman, comedian, or a preacher?"

And in some cases, they may be right!

But I was going to go for it. Just like the preacher said, sometimes, you need to move when the spirit says move, and you need to obey when he says *do*.

I did know that when God wants to get something done, he will get it done; if he told you to do it and you don't, then he will find someone else.

I, right then and there, decided to act on the moment, to seize the day if you will, just as the preacher had.

Maybe someone else was supposed to get this word from the preacher, but I stepped up and received it from him. Maybe somebody else could have written it better than I.

Probably so, there is always someone stronger, faster, better, or smarter; but I stepped up and claimed it as mine.

I passed security, telling them that I was the author he had called out. They escorted me up to him, and I introduced myself.

I said, "My name is Dana Solla, and I am an author. You said—"

He interrupted me in mid-sentence and said, "Good you must be the one, God told me to give you a message."

I was really quite shocked at the moment and honestly very nervous; I don't know why, I just was.

Now to hear from this man saying he had a message from God for me, I felt a little scared of all that. I thought, "What have I gotten myself into now. God has a message for me, what if I can't do it?"

And that is the whole point, I can't do it by myself; it is only through him that I am able to do any of it at all. Anyone who would know me would know this to be true and know it had to be a God thing because this guy can't do it by himself.

He went on to say, "God says that you are, for the next ten days, to wake up an hour earlier, go on a fast, and pray in a quite place, just you and him. When you have finished praying, you need to journal what God has said to you. From the journal you write, you are to write a book and call it Ten Hours with God."

He then started to walk away with the senior pastor.

He said as he departed, "God bless you, and it will be a best seller if you do what God said do."

And he left.

I did do what he said do, and I did pray and fast. I did journal and keep a log of my conversations with God. I have been obedient to what I believe God has called for me to do, be that good, bad, or indifferent. Whether it will be a best seller or not, that is not my department; marketing and sales is God's part of this partnership.

My job was to write and write the best that I could. I feel that I have honored my commitment to God, and I know that God's word does not come back void.

The intent of this book is to be a personal testimony as to learning to walk in the gift that God has given each of us. To recognize what that gift is and how to develop it so that you may be able to do what it is that has always been in your heart.

I pray that no matter what age you are, this book can help you find that peace and joy in your life that only comes with fulfilling the call that God has put on your life.

I pray that the young may be able to understand God's gifts through a blessing rather than learning the lessons the hard way.

For those that are older and have learned these lessons the hard way, know that it is never too late to step into the calling that God has for you. Your joy and happiness is just a matter of discovering and doing what it is that God said to do—the fulfillment of your purpose.

It has taken me more than fifty years to learn this, and I have never felt more contented.

I give you the same instructions that were given to me.

For the next ten days, get up an hour earlier than normal, find a quite place, pray and fast, and spend an hour with God.

When you come out from your hour with God, write down has God spoken to you. Use the blank pages at the end of each chapter to compose your ten hours with God.

Even if you feel that nothing happened or was said, I assure that something did. You will see as the days go by, so have faith and know that God is communicating with you. Be diligent and stay true to it all the way through, and you will see the result. It is in God's timing, so be patient with yourself and God.

During this time, wear on your left wrist a green, three-strand braided cord, symbolizing being tied to God—green being the color of wisdom and growth.

King Solomon speaks of things that are meaningless and have no real value. He says: In the book of Ecclesiastes 4:8-12 (KJV)

There is one alone, and there is not a second; yea, he hath neither child nor brother: yet is there no end of all his labour; neither is his eye satisfied with riches; neither saith he, For whom do I labour, and bereave my soul of good? This is also vanity, yea, it is a sore travail. Two are better than one; because they have a good reward for their labour. For if they fall, the one will lift up his fellow: but woe to him that is alone when he falleth; for he hath not another to help him up. Again, if two lie together, then they have heat: but how can one be warm alone?And if one prevail against him, two shall withstand him; and a threefold cord is not quickly broken.

I refer to this scripture for the purpose of you being interwoven, tied together with, and bound to God. Each strand will represent one part: 1.) God, 2.) you, 3.) your purpose.

At the end of the ten days, give a copy of this book to someone else that you would like to bless.

Visit our website, www.forapurposeministries.com, and let us know of your personal encounter with Jesus.

I GIVE YOU
TEN HOURS WITH GOD

I PRAY

I believe God answers prayers, and prayer does change things.

Know the difference when a prayer is answered and when it is not.

Many of us lose confidence in prayer because we do not recognize the answer.

We ask for strength, and God gives us challenges to overcome, which makes us strong.

We pray for wisdom, and God gives us choices, the results of which develops wisdom.

We pray for prosperity, and God gives us a brain and brawn to work.

We pray for courage, and God gives us danger to overcome.

We ask for favors, and God gives us opportunities.

I pray for many reasons. I pray to worship God. It is written: "Thou shalt worship the Lord thy God and no other," the first of the Ten Commandments, and that God loves to be worshipped. So I pray to worship God.

I pray for a personal relationship with God and an ear to hear his voice, to develop a bond, a covenant, between us so that I may be able to count on him and him me. So I pray!

I pray to give God praise. I praise God because it is written: "He is worthy of all praise," and God loves to be praised. God has angels in heaven that fly around his glorious throne twenty-four hours a day and seven days a week, singing, "Hallelujah! Hallelujah! Is the highest praise of all," and that is their job, to praise God! So I pray to praise God.

I pray to give thanks to God. I thank him for everything, for without him, I would have nothing. I give God thanks for everything he has done, for that which he is doing, and for those things he is yet to do. Even though his work is complete, mine is not.

The things that he has done have only made me ready for those things that he is doing. Those things that are being done only make me ready for those things that he is yet to do. God loves to be thanked. So I pray to give God thanks.

I pray to be close to God. I want our relationship to grow, and I want to hear what he has to say to me about anything and everything I do. I know I can do nothing, nothing that really matters, without him, so I wait to hear God's voice on all matters. So I pray! I pray for understanding.

I want God's guidance; I want his favor, and I want his blessing. So I pray!

I don't want to do anything on my own any more and be outside of God's will. I have done that too many times in my past and made such a mess of things that it scares me to think that I would do it again. Maybe that's what it meant "to have fear of God." Because you know that anything you can do, he can do better. No matter how good your stuff is, his is better. After all, how do the universe, the world, and everything in it that you made compare to the universe and the world God has already created? It's kind of like when God asked Job, "Where were you when I created the heavens and the earth?"

I fear not being under God's covering or having my heart tuned to something other than what God's heart is in tune with. To me, fear is doing something that doesn't have God's covering or blessing attached to it; it is being outside of his will and outside of his presence. That's scary! It is something to be afraid of. So I pray! I pray for courage.

Sometimes when I pray, I find myself in a still and quite place trying to hear a still, small voice. Sometimes I think I hear it, sometimes I don't hear anything at all, and sometimes I think that it's only my imagination playing tricks on me. But I think we all do that, I wonder if what we are doing is really prayer or pretend. I believe that this is the part when faith comes into play. It is written that the only way to please God is through faith. I believe that when we use our faith, God uses his grace; when we have his grace, we qualify for his mercy.

The Apostle Paul said in 2 Corinthians 12:9 (KJV)

9And he said unto me, My grace is sufficient for thee: for my strength is made perfect in weakness. Most gladly therefore will I rather glory in my infirmities, that the power of Christ may rest upon me.

So I pray. I pray for grace and mercy.

I pray every morning with my wife, and I pray with her before we go to sleep every night. I take the kids to school in the mornings; and we, the kids and I, call my wife from the car while she is at work to pray for a covering over them everyday. I have one of the kids lead the prayer each day. At first, they thought that it was silly and didn't know what to say, but as I lead them by my example, they took it up pretty quickly. Now they just break into a prayer without hesitation. They pray for traveling mercies, protection over their school day, and blessings on their studies. They pray for our family and friends and any special things going on at the time. It has now become a habit, so much so that they question when we get close to the school and we haven't prayed yet. We pray to put a covering of protection over them and to be a blessing to someone and expect miracles. We are the inheritors of the promise and blessings through Abraham, the blessings of prosperity, abundance, and faith. If we look toward God as a source for all our needs and as long as we walk in it and keep the covenant that God made with Abraham, then we keep the promise of his blessing. So I pray. I pray for favor.

There was a story told by my wife to us about a woman that used to sit outside of her school twice a day. My wife worked at a local elementary school. The lady sat outside in front of the school in the morning when the children came to school and after school when they left to go home at the days end.

She looked like any other woman that came to drop her kids off at school, nothing really very special or out of the ordinary about her. She was in her mid-thirties and looked just like your neighbor. She drove a minivan and parked just up the street from the drop-off zone. In the mornings, she stood outside the van in a white terry cloth robe she got from a luxury resort hotel while on vacation with a newspaper folded up in the side pocket, a pair of SpongeBob slippers, and a cup of coffee from the convenience store in the corner. She watched as the children passed by her walking through the gates into the school yard.

In the afternoons, she came early to get a good parking spot again, just up the street from the pickup zone. She would wear everyday house clothes in a very casual way and just seemed to belong there. She smiled and said hello to those that would walk by, and even knew some of the kids and parents by name; a very friendly type, not conspicuous or loud; never really bringing attention to herself, but always there.

This woman that sat outside the school was a confessed witch, and her purpose was to cast spells over the school and see if any of the children reacted to her spells. If they did she would have others, children and parents who were part of her coven, approach these kids and further their actions by feeding into the spirit that was on them.

The spells she was casting were of hostility and disobedience, even promoting violence on the campus.

The kids would offer those that wanted it cigarettes and drugs from weed to cocaine, meth, and all kinds of other stuff to take before school even started. If they could get them to skip class or not even go to school at all, they considered it a great victory.

She later confessed that there were some who were so easy to recognize by their demeanor; she could pick them out pretty readily after watching them for only a very short while. She also said that she had other witches in her coven who were stationed at other schools in the area doing the same thing and they would talk to each other about some of the kids they had targeted.

She remarked one time how easy it was because nobody ever thought to question her as to why she was there. She and the other witches used to laugh about it and called it a turkey shoot.

This was very scary to us because of the stark reality and the truth of the situation. Everybody saw her but didn't know the real reason why she was there. They only thought that she was dropping off her own children in the morning or picking them up in the afternoon just like everybody else; nobody thought the wiser.

We learn in church and through the study of God's word that we are in a spiritual battle every day against powers and principalities, fallen angels and their minions, and certainly, witches who are practiced in the black arts. Their purpose is but to rob, steal, and to kill. So I pray! I pray for discernment.

With our children being so innocent and vulnerable, so susceptible in trusting others, especially those that are around our schools, it startles us awake to a common truth, that our children are a high priority to Satan and at great risk every day. They are targeted and individually picked out because of the spirit that is on them when we leave and go on our way, leaving them to deal with whatever is there for them to deal with. We think that it is just the four Rs: readin', writen' and 'rithmetic. If you think that way, then you fail.

The spirit that is on the children is the spirit we place as parents when they leave our presence, the spirit of anger or depression or the spirit of confusion and abuse. The last words that come out of our mouths when they leave from us are the spirits that stay with them throughout the day; these words carry with them the spirit of a blessing or a curse. What words come out of your mouth when your children leave from your presence? So I pray! I pray for blessings.

There are generational curses being passed down from us to our children and are reinforced everyday, and we don't even realize it. We just blindly go from place to place, never giving it a second thought, thinking that these things may be true but they don't really touch us and it can't be that bad. We don't really see it for what it is, and that is the strength of the enemy, keeping it in the dark and on the down low until all of a sudden, it explodes and it's too late to save them or any other victims from their actions.

As long as we fail to recognize them for what they are or don't believe that sort of thing is even happening, we have a problem as it strengthens these demonic forces; and they think we are easy prey. We are the hunted and the real game they seek as trophies.

We are so locked into what it is that we are doing that we fail to see the big picture and the real battles in life.

We are so busy struggling to meet deadlines and keep appointments, trying to pay our bills, or getting our own free time that we neglected to see what is really important; how to steward over our children and bringing them up in God's word, teaching them to survive and prosper in the world is found in the Holy Bible.

Like the acronym BIBLE

B- basic

I- instructions

B- before

L- leaving

E- earth

God gave us stewardship over these children as a gift in our lives. We understand the words, and we love our children and do what we have been taught. But herein lays the dilemma, how do we do the right thing for our children and ourselves? So I pray! I pray for wisdom.

Our parents may have meant well, so we try to pattern ourselves after them; or they didn't do so well, and we declare that we will never be like them. All the while, these are the devil's playground: our hearts, our minds, and our thoughts. And he is after our souls.

If he can attack our souls, then it's an open door to our faith. He knows that if he can break our faith, then he can break us. For without faith, we have no hope; and with no hope, we die. So we must guard our hearts, our minds, and our thoughts and say, "Not on my watch."

We need to learn and be aware of the truth behind the veil of the physical world and recognize the truth in the spiritual world. So I pray! I pray for truth.

These things happen in front of our children's schools everyday too. Did you know this? When you think about it, it should shock the hell out of you! And make you aware that this battle is all around us all the time and our children are at great risk. we need to know this so that we can steward over them properly and protect them.

We know when someone is hit or knocked down that there is something happening that we need to be aware of, we can see it. The same is true for the spiritual world. Even when we cannot see it, we need to cover our children with prayer and dispatch God's angels to watch over and protect them. The enemy uses the element of time to his advantage. Things get dull with time, and as it passes, their importance seems to wane. If it doesn't hurt too much, then we just get used to it and adjust to the discomfort. Slowly but surely, it builds up until eventually you wonder, "How did it ever get this bad and when did it happen?"

We search our memory and can't put a finger on any one thing. That's because it is just one thing! One thing at a time added up together becomes an accumulation of things over a period of time and then bam! It's staring at us in the face and using our state of shock against us. This is how the enemy works, and the reason why we cannot do anything about it by ourselves. We need God and the blood of Jesus to cover us. So I pray! I pray for mercy.

Think of it like this and visualize in your mind: A soldier standing watch, posted at a gate, a portal. A changing of the guard is taking place. You approach your brother in arms, and you see that the enemy is approaching him from behind. You call out to warn your comrade and tell him that the enemy is sneaking up on him. The enemy hears you, ducks, and takes cover.

The soldier, however, says that nothing is there. Now you know what you saw, and you know the enemy is closing in on him. So you call out to warn the soldier again, yet the soldier denies that there is anyone there.

The enemy hears the soldier's denial and becomes a little bolder now and comes out from hiding and continues to stalk the soldier. You see the enemy again. This time, he is right behind the soldier with a knife out and ready to grab the soldier and overpower him.

You again warn the soldier. "The enemy is right behind you. He has his knife out and is inches away from killing you."

The enemy ducks and tries to hide again, but the soldier doesn't even turn around to look. He just says that there is nothing there to worry about and he is fine. The enemy now feels completely confident that this soldier is doomed and he can take him out without fear of being caught or being discovered by the soldier.

There is nothing you can do. He doesn't heed your warnings, and he doesn't believe you. So you watch as the inevitable happens. The enemy completes his mission and takes out the unbelieving soldier, killing him.

You blame yourself for not being closer or earlier, for not saying the right thing to prevent it from happening.

You carry the lie of guilt with you for the rest of your life, and by doing so, the enemy will have two victims. So I pray! I pray for protection.

This happens every day, all around, and all the time. The enemy is sneaking up on your children right in front of your face and is counting on you to think that it is something other than what it really is—spiritual warfare. The enemy is trying to get you to think that this isn't even happening, to get you into a state of denial. Open your eyes and pay attention to what is really going on around you!

What are you going to do when somebody tells you that your children are being attacked, and they need you right away, and if you don't hurry, they are going to be killed?

Are you going to be like the soldier and say that there really is nothing there to be afraid of?

Watch and see what happens when your kids turn to drugs or alcohol, turn into gangbangers or thieves and murders. What then?

Are you going to say you didn't see it coming or that you didn't even know what was going on? Are you going to blame their surroundings, or the times in which they are being brought up, or say, "Kids will be kids, it's just a phase that they are going through, and they will grow out it"?

What if it's not, and what if they don't? What then? Are you going to be going to their funerals and having a car wash to pay for it? Or are you going to get up and rush to their aid as fast as you can? So I pray! I pray for vision.

This witch that hung around the school came to light because she confessed on her own. Her spells weren't working on some of the kids, and she couldn't understand why. One of her neighbors and she had been talking, the neighbor was a Christian believer and told the witch that they prayed over their children everyday. The neighbor had no idea that this lady was a witch; and over a period of time, the witch tried even harder to cast spells over the Christian neighbor's children. Nothing took, as a matter of fact, the spells reversed and went back upon the witch herself.

When that happened, the witch went back over to the Christian neighbor's house to ask her about the prayers she was praying over her children.

When the neighbor told her that she was a member of a women's prayer group and that there were seven women that prayed every day at 5:30 a.m., she confessed that she was a witch and told her how the spells had been reversed and sent back upon her. She subsequently asked if the neighbor would pray for her. The witch, or should I say ex-witch, wanted to join in with these other women and become a part of their prayer group. They didn't let her in right away because you never know the tricks of the enemy, but they did pray for and about her. She did, very shortly afterwards, move away from there and started attending church, where she gave her life over to Jesus.

But she did confess to trying to cast spells on the children and had been doing so for years. So I pray! I pray covering.

My wife and I pray several times during the course of the day and as the need may arise, and the need arises a lot! We know that prayer changes things; we know that prayer makes a difference. I know when something comes up, and I pray about it. I make better decisions.

What prayer does is put us in that place where we constantly seek God; this is a direct communication with Father God. I learned to tune my ears to the sound of his voice. I learned to have a dialog with him, and I know he gives better advice than I do. I have learned to trust in him, and even be patient and not get frustrated when things don't happen in my timing, which is usually a good thing for me.

Spending time alone with God sounds like such an easy and simple thing to do—when really it's not. All kinds of things come up in your everyday life, and there are many reasons for you to find something else to do.

To seek God and spend quality time with Him takes a consistent effort and dedication. I think God makes it that way to see how serious we are when calling on him and how serious he needs to take us. If we don't take him seriously, why should he take us seriously?

According to Romans 12:3, KJV, Paul says, "Through the grace given unto me; to every man that is among you not to think of himself more highly than he ought to think, but to think soberly, according as God hath dealt to every man the measure of faith." Romans 12:6, KJV, says: "Having then gifts differing according to the grace that is given to us, whether prophecy, let us prophesy according to the portion of faith."

Both measured out in equal proportion are his grace and his mercy. So I pray! I pray to be proven.

His grace is being measured out when we don't even deserve it—when good things happen to us and we know we have done nothing on our own to deserve it. When you have God's grace, you are truly blessed, and what else could you possibly need? If God is for you then who could be against you?

Then comes His mercy, mercy gives us forgiveness when we deserve far worse treatment than we received. All of this becomes clearer as we spend dedicated time with God—one-on-one, in relationship, speaking with each other, communicating.

Communication only takes place when there is a dialogue, and a dialogue consists of one speaking and the other listening, then the roles reverse. Conversation consists of many elements—good, bad and, indifferent. The mere fact that communication exists proves the relationship and the desire for that relationship. So I pray! I pray for relationship.

I spend much time communicating with God. But to be honest with myself, I need to spend much more time, be more patient and persistent and more dedicated in seeking Him—and not just for his advice and what he can do for me, but for more time to be close to Him Just because!

Wouldn't it be just so cool to hang out with God for no other reason than you like Him? Because you want to and you like his company, I do. Besides, I can trust him. So I pray! I pray to spend time with God.

To be in a relationship with God sometimes seems difficult to do. God puts a believer through test after test.

These tests never end; they continue at all levels of one's relationship with God. They are always about our faith.

When put to the test, I believe God makes us prove our words to Him —and that is the test. One may say they believe in God for a certain thing and profess their love for God but while in the midst of their petition, God says, "Prove it to me!"

God wants proof and evidence of the love that is being declared to Him. It's like God is almost saying, "If you say you love me, then prove it."

Scripture says,

> John 14:15 (KJV)
>
> If ye love me, keep my commandments.

> John 15:10 (KJV)
>
> If ye keep my commandments, ye shall abide in my love; even as I have kept my Father's commandments, and abide in his love.

So he puts out a thing for you to confirm, your love for him. It always is a test of faith. That is why Jesus said in Matthew 17:20 (KJV)

And Jesus said unto them, Because of your unbelief: for verily I say unto you, If ye have faith as a grain of mustard seed, ye shall say unto this mountain, Remove hence to yonder place; and it shall remove; and nothing shall be impossible unto you.

The tests are always a matter of the depth of our faith. It always comes down to how much we trust in him; that is, the removal of yourself from a situation and our complete dependence on God as to who gets the credit and the recognition for the work and the outcome.

Do you do it with your own understanding, or is it all about God? Because God is not a respecter of people nor can any flesh be glorified before Him. He wants to know how obedient we are and if we mean what we say when we say "I love you, Lord!"

Look what He did with Job, Abraham, Isaac, and Jacob and what Joseph and Moses did to prove their love; when Abraham was told by God to take his son, Isaac, away and sacrifice him, it was a test of Abraham's faith.

But as the story went on, God did not require that Abraham complete the act of the sacrifice. If He had, He would not have been able to keep his promise to Abraham, the promise that he would be the father of many nations, that his seed would be more than the sands on the seashore. And that would have made God a liar. If He would have lied, then He couldn't be God; as a matter of fact, God stopped him and had put a ram in the bush as a replacement.

God would not let Abraham sacrifice his son; God went so far as to replace the sacrifice of a son with His own son, and let us not forget what Jesus did to prove His love!

All the sacrifices they were asked to prove how much trust and faith each of them had in the Father, what did each do to show how much they were willing to trust God so that God may be magnified?

They each committed all of their lives and all of their hearts to God. What promise has God made to you?

Have you given all of your heart and all of your life to Him? So I pray! I pray to fulfill promise.

For each of them, they clearly backed up what they said with their very lives; they proved their faith. God wants to know if the words "I, me, or mine" are at the basis of what it is that you do. Truly, in your heart of hearts way deep down inside, can you honestly say that you don't want some recognition for what you have done?

Come on and be honest now. Not even a little bit? It's really not just a matter of giving over to Him, but a matter as to whether we do it cheerfully. The Lord loves a cheerful giver! Don't do it because you think you are supposed to or you are expected to; that's the wrong heart in giving, and God doesn't want what we reluctantly give. He wants our best, with all of our heart, given cheerfully.

Do it because you want to, do it because you are glad to, do it because you are grateful He is there and willing to take it from you and it is pleasing to Him. Be glad that you don't have to carry that thing around with you anymore.

So I pray! I pray for God's acceptance.

God is a jealous God, and the first commandment says that you shall worship no other god before him. That includes *yourself*—no matter how humble you think you are or how humble you make others think you are. No flesh can glory before or after God, and He is no respecter of persons. God wants *all* the glory, and He deserves it. So again I ask, are you a cheerful giver?

Do you give God all the glory and all the praise? God will be happy to pour out blessings unto us so that we may prosper and enjoy the life that He has given us.

What you give in private, God will reward openly. So I pray! I pray to give honor to God.

Don't be like Moses when God asks you, "Who gave them the water?". (Speaking of the children of Israel in the wilderness thirsting again, showing no patience or faith because God had given them water once before by Moses striking his staff against a rock.) Reply "I did," it just might keep you out of the promised land! You may have been the one who struck your staff on the rock, and water may have come out from hence; yet know the truth, God is the one that made the water come forth. So I pray! I pray for the promise.

Once we have learned how to give, quietly and in private, cheerfully and with joy, we need to learn how to receive. Reaping is receiving the harvest. The laws of reaping and sowing, giving and receiving are found in God's word and harvesting the fruit is the blessings that God gives openly.

It may seem a little funny to think that we need to learn how to receive, but it is true. Most of us really don't know how to receive, even if it is in the form of a compliment or some kind of recognition.

We tend to say that we are better at giving to others in need than receiving; we don't know how to accept something that is given freely to us.

Did you ever stop to think that God is offended or saddened when he tries to give us something, and we won't accept it? What did God do to you for you to have insulted him this way? When he tried to give you a gift because he loves you, you turn it down. Is he a bad God, is he not good?

We need to learn how to receive when God wants to bless us because He does love us.

How would you feel if you saved all your money to get your child a very special gift and when it came, time for you to give it to them, they just said "No, I don't want it. Give it to someone else," and they set it down and walked away?

Being a cheerful giver and a cheerful receiver is pleasing to God; it shows Him that you have proper perspective and balance in these matters. It shows that you recognize His hand at work, you appreciate what He has done for you, and that you have faith in Him. So I pray! I pray to be a cheerful receiver of God's gifts and blessings.

I pray and fast for spiritual health, to break the hold of generational curses and familiar spirits.

> Jesus said in Mark 9:29-29 (KJV)
>
> And when he was come into the house, his disciples asked him privately, Why could not we cast him out?And he said unto them, This kind can come forth by nothing, but by prayer and fasting.

I pray and fast with a specific purpose in mind and a specific outcome that I expect to be loosed on the earth. So I pray! I pray to God.

I pray by myself, and I pray with others corporately. I pray for you.

Journal
First Hour
I Pray

_____
_____
_____
_____
_____
_____
_____
_____
_____
_____
_____
_____
_____
_____
_____
_____
_____
_____
_____
_____
_____
_____
_____
_____

I FAST

We bow down our heads and call a fast as an acceptable day of the Lord!

The book of Isaiah from the Old Testament speaks of "fasting" for many different reasons and many different purposes. Like the spokes of a wheel, the reasons we fast are held together by a band, a circle surrounding and connecting them all together leading to a hub. The hub of fasting is our relationship with God and wanting to be closer to him. For each reason that we fast, we purpose God's intervention, support, or clarity in the matters of our lives—that the Holy Spirit guides us and we may better understand how to be all God has called us to be and to walk in the purpose that God has called for us.

To demonstrate with the purpose, we can set our flesh aside and make obvious to God our submission to his will—to have his favor, his mercy, his grace, and his blessing in our lives—making a clear and loud choice of seeking him and doing the things needed to prove ourselves worthy to receive that for which we petition.

The Prophet Isaiah also said: Isaiah 58:6 (KJV)

Is not this the fast that I have chosen? to loose the bands of wickedness, to undo the heavy burdens, and to let the oppressed go free, and that ye break every yoke?

Jeremiah proclaimed a fast before the Lord to all the people of Jerusalem.

Jeremiah 36:9 (KJV)

And it came to pass in the fifth year of Jehoiakim the son of Josiah king of Judah, in the ninth month, that they proclaimed a fast before the Lord to all the people in Jerusalem, and to all the people that came from the cities of Judah unto Jerusalem.

Joel 1:14 (KJV)

Sanctify ye a fast, call a solemn assembly, gather the elders and all the inhabitants of the land into the house of the Lord your God, and cry unto the Lord,

Jonah 3:5 (KJV)

So the people of Nineveh believed God, and proclaimed a fast, and put on sackcloth, from the greatest of them even to the least of them that they may not perish

This is the power of fasting and the impact that it has. I fast for health: spiritual, emotional and physical.

I fast for spiritual health to get closer to God, to hear God's voice and His council on matters in my life. Sometimes, on matters that are very serious and important to me—on relationships, parenting, and professional issues; sometimes, just because I need to be renewed and kept fresh; and sometimes, in preparation for an upcoming activity and I want to be at my very best, that all of my senses are in tune and ready to perform—both physical and spiritual.

Fasting is intended to crucify the flesh. In other words, to deny the fleshly desires and interest of this world, to bring the flesh under the control of the will and the Spirit of God, with the intention of bringing those things that are of the spiritual world into this physical world.

The flesh, by nature, has an uncontrollable appetite; it is unquenchable and can run wild if left unchecked. The flesh must be trained to submit to the control of its director, me and you, as we are spiritual beings residing in these physical bodies—the temple of God, a place where the Holy Spirit is to reside. Otherwise, we become a prisoner to our wants and desires, a slave to what it is that we think we physically need; we work for it rather than putting our flesh to work for us. It is a matter of training.

This is the realm of addictions; other spirits use the flesh as a portal into our lives. The flesh is susceptible to what it likes without thinking of consequences. Consequences are the results of the actions and the choices that are taken. The human being is an addiction-prone creature; we can become addicted to anything, and we do. Many people think that they aren't addicted to anything, but I submit that we all are addicted to more than one thing. Most of us are addicted to several things and don't even know it.

For example, we become addicted to such things as the obvious: drugs, alcohol, pornography, food, money, and gambling. And the not so obvious: things such as work and careers, we're not happy unless we are working all the time. Things like TV, we come home from work, to our comfortable surroundings, just to watch a TV program, from sports to sitcoms and soap operas. We are addicted to shopping, we buy things when we feel good and when we don't feel so good, even when we can't afford them, and we hide them from our spouses. It may cause us financial hardship, yet we still do it. Some people are addicted to recognition, we are not happy unless we are recognized for something that we have done. Not just recognized, we need a major production from those around us, to give us fanfares, parades, and balloons, by needing to hear over and over how well we have done, how good we are, and how right we are. And if it is not done the appropriate number of times, then we have an attitude. These all come from feelings of inadequacies and lack within ourselves.

Some people are addicted to being right, they will argue and battle to prove how right they are, even when they know they're wrong. They need to understand and categorize everything, file it away, find a place where it logically belongs.

Addictions come in many forms and many disguises; they are the things that we run to, to celebrate or run away from, to hide when the world gets too close and personal.

We sometimes sleep ourselves away from an issue that is causing us discomfort, or we have a cigarette and a drink.

We are spiritual creatures living in this earthly realm and must use our physicality to move about in this place. We are supposed to use our bodies, our physicality, for the purposes of which God has ordained for us. Lord, let me be your eyes, ears, mouth, hands, and feet. Set my heart after your own heart. We are not to be led by our physical nature. If we are led by our physical nature, it leads us into sin, self-destruction, and certain death.

If we look at the flesh as an animal that we send forth to do our bidding, it does what we will it do, like a dog that we train to fetch. We throw a ball or a stick to a dog and tell the dog to go get it and bring it back, and we repeat the process over and over until the dog tires us out.

In life, it is much the same way. If we want a job, we send the flesh out to get it. It must be trained on what job we want it to get. If we don't train it, then it brings back the first and only kind of job it can find. This leaves us dissatisfied and angry because we are not doing what it is that we are called to do. We feel we have no purpose, no value. We covet those things that others have, of whom we believe are following their purpose. If we admire them and try to make their purpose our own, then again, we are left unfulfilled, for a life without purpose is a life wasted. And none of us wants to feel that our lives are a waste. We know in our subconscious that it isn't right, and we become angry about it and inevitably become destructive toward ourselves and others.

This concept is very important to grasp. To be able to wrap your arms around and understand, it will help to see some of the areas where we have shortcomings and know why we behave the way we do. It will also help us to see why others behave the way they do, which can lead to the path of forgiving them a trespass and understanding why they did what they did. It doesn't mean that they aren't to be held accountable for their actions. What it means is that we can look past the action, see them for who they are or what they are lacking, and why they acted the way they did. This understanding helps us see a soul that is in lack and hurting. It can help us to have compassion for our brothers and sisters, sons and daughters.

To illustrate the point, one might be able to relate to this:

If a young man was to have grown up in a single-parent home, maybe just a mother. Perhaps the father left home when the boy was young through a divorce, or even had died. Whatever the case, the boy grew up without a father figure in the home. The mother, who may have been a praying mother, brought the boy up with a Christian foundation. But the boy still went astray, committed a crime and finds himself in prison. This young man may, at that time, find regret and remorse for his actions. A spirit that was on him had kept him blind and thinking that what he was doing was okay. He felt his actions were justified. But at the time he committed the crimes, he was doing what was popular with his peers—either to be popular or a way to make money but still trying to carve a piece of something out for himself. That spirit has now departed, the assignment has been completed, its mission accomplished. Other spirits now come to replace it as it hands in its charge to them. The young man has had his future stolen from him, his life in ruins, his family left heartbroken and wondering what will happen now.

He is left sitting on the edge of the cold, hard, cement slab that holds his thin and lumpy mattress, what he is supposed to call his bed for the next how many years. A cell door made of steel slams shut with a loud thud, echoing its sound as the other doors follow in sequence like dominos. He can hear the sounds of the other inmates as they settle in for what is about to be the first in a long line of restless and sleepless nights for him. He sits with his elbows on his knees and holding his forehead in his hands. He starts to weep, but he can't let the others hear him because it would be taken as a sign of weakness, and in here any sign of weakness could mean your life. There are predators that are up in this place, waiting to see where your weakness is so that they can get over on you. As he sits in this cold, dank, and gray place, he starts thinking finally with a clear mind, and reality has set in. He is able to see and realize that what he was doing wasn't worth it, that he was chasing the wind and trying to grasp a vapor. He realizes that you can't do that, you can't hold on to a mist. Chasing things glorified on the earth that have no lasting value is all folly and done in vanity. You can't take them to jail with you for comfort.

He thinks of how he used to make fun of the old man that used to live across the street and go to work at what he thought was a do-nothing, waste-of-time job every day. He thinks of how the old man used to say how he was satisfied doing what he did, even if people didn't think it was the most important job or that others had authority over him, that some people made a lot more money and had nicer cars and more things. But he and his wife had been married thirty-five years, their house was paid for, he had no debt, and he didn't owe anybody anything. He said that he ate well, and he had a sweet sleep. That he enjoyed what he did, and it was a gift from God. That it is a man's heritage to labor and to find joy in his labor because it is a gift from God.

He remembers a time when he was just a boy of twelve years. He was invited to the old man's grandson's thirteenth birthday party. He and the other boy had become friends and would play when he came to visit his grandfather. At the party, the old man celebrated with his grandson in front of everyone, singing his praises all day long and even gave him a new bike to ride when he came to visit. This young man didn't have a father figure in the house. His dad had moved out years ago. After the party, he went home and was missing his father. He wanted to experience some of what his friend just had. So he asked his mother if he could call his father. When he called, his father answered the phone but didn't have time for him and told him that he had caught him at bad time; it seemed every time he called, it was a bad time. His dad told him not to call back, that he would call him when he had the time.

The boy found himself sitting on the edge of the bed, with his face in his hands, crying. When his mother came to comfort him, he became very angry; and that's when he made an inner vow that he would never let his emotions get the better of him again and that if he couldn't get the recognition from those close to him, he would take it from others. He didn't care if it hurt them; as a matter of fact, if it did, he got more pleasure from it. At least it wasn't him that was hurting. Now they could know his pain and suffering.

So there he sat, in the same position all those years ago after his friend's birthday party, on the edge of his bed with his face in his hands. A lie robbed this growing boy of his future, stole from him just like he had stolen and robbed from all those others that he thought were suckers, stupid, and weak. How he used to think he had it all figured out, how he was so much smarter than everybody else, it all came so easily, and he thought he could continue to get away with it. He had gotten away with things for so long. He thought that he was untouchable, that things just rolled off of him like water off a duck, and that nothing could stick to him, as if he were made of Teflon.

A lie blinded him into thinking that all these other people who he played over and over again were the stupid ones. *Now look at you, who is the stupid one now?* he thinks to himself.

He finally has the blinders off and can see with clarity that the things his mother had said were right, even when he couldn't wait to get out the front door to go be with his friends, saying to himself, "Here she goes again, praying over me and in front of my friends. How embarrassing." The excuses he would have to give to his friends for his mother's behavior.

As he sits in that cell, he wishes he could have had the life of that simple old man that just found joy in what it was that he was doing. He didn't care if it was all that; he just found joy in it because that is what God had given for him to do. It was a gift; there was an invitation of satisfaction and fulfillment in it, and he could eat and drink and sleep a sweet sleep.

He had something to leave his children's children. He could leave them a legacy of hard work, and righteous living has its own reward—the wages of right living before God.

Now this young man was receiving the wages he was due for as he satup in that cell. He was never taught how to be a man. He had uncles that spent time with him when they could. His mom sometimes had a boyfriend but didn't want to have anybody around that might cause a problem for the kids, so she raised them by herself, denying herself from dating. And when she finally found somebody she loved and wanted to bring into the family, the young man rebels and becomes violent, angry, and attacks the man.

Now, he can see what a grave mistake he made. Does he get angrier and become worse? Or does he turn to God, repent, seek forgiveness, and do something to make up for the deeds that he had done?

God has given him an invitation of forgiveness and healing. Will he accept it?

For you who were wronged by this young man, can you forgive him for what he has done to you and the damage he caused in your life and to your property? Can you forgive because "they know not what they do"?

If the remorse and regret are sincere and if he is able to repent from these sins, he still can be saved and have a new future created. If not, he will still be blinded by the attack of other demon spirits that come to finish the job the first demon spirit started.

He may have heard about what the right and wrong things were, he may have been told the proper way to behave and treat others, but there was no one there to teach him. No one to stand up and teach him how a boy becomes a man; no one to step up with the authority that a young man needs to learn how to respect people and insure he doesn't run all over everybody because he's physically capable of doing so. He didn't have anyone other than the world to teach him that it isn't just your physical power that you use to get your way. The world's lessons are harsh. This young man doesn't know how to act or behave; and he is forced to act in some kind of way, so he accepts the ways of the world. By then, it was too late. The world has a false promise of glitter and glory that the young man finds hard to resist because he doesn't know anything.

Can we see past the actions and see the broken young man that is suffering because he just didn't know? He rejected the teachings that a praying mother tried to give him, teachings from church people, and even pastors he called hypocrites because they couldn't walk on water. Never giving anybody credit for waking up every day and doing their best, overcoming the same battles he is facing. Not heeding their advice or listening to some of their own victories or failures. There was no one there to teach him, and these are the consequences of his choices.

We are all responsible for our actions, and the bible is very clear about that. We will all be held accountable, and ignorance is no excuse.

Yet can we find compassion for someone who would repent and forgiveness for someone who would accept God's invitation?

Or a daughter that grows up in the same kind of environment and turns to drugs and alcohol or prostitutes herself—gives herself away and becomes promiscuous. She is out for recognition and acceptance. She tries to find love in a place that there is no love, only being used and abused. She misunderstands what real love is, and this behavior causes her to slip and fall. It opens a door for other spirits to come, a place where the Holy Spirit is supposed to be. When other spirits enter in, it is not the person committing these acts but rather the spirit that resides in them that cause the behavior. And it is the intention of those spirits to cause these young people to fall, to lose their souls. They come but to lie, steal, destroy, and kill.

If we can see this, then we can see past the spirit in them and know that they know not what they do!

It puts us on the path of finding a way to forgive them; we forgive them for they know not what they do!

If we can understand this and really see it for what it is, then we will not fall into the mindset of getting revenge. The best way for us to deal with this kind of thing is to pray, fast, and glorify God. Forgive them their trespasses and teach them that God has a better way. The devil hates that!

Knowing that God has a way of making things right, nobody gets away with anything. For every action we take, for every decision that we make, there is a consequence, a price to pay. If he committed a crime, then he must do the time. If she had sex and got pregnant, then she will have a baby. Or she tries to run away from the consequences of her actions and decides to have an abortion, then that is a consequence she can never run away from. These are the things that God makes you deal with for the decisions that you make. The good news is that he is there to forgive you and make you a new creature, to use what you have been through as a lesson to you and to others.

The misery that you go through is the ministry that you are called to.

If we can understand this concept, then it can help us to see where some of the attitudes we have came from and see the better to forgive ourselves for the mistakes that we have made.

The only way to find your purpose in life is to have God reveal it to you through prayer and fasting. If you haven't found what your purpose in life is, it could be that the spirit of laziness has taken a stronghold over your life, when you should or could be doing something but find reasons not to.

Prayer and fasting can break this spiritual stronghold and change your life once you find your purpose. When we want food, we send the flesh out to get it. We train the flesh on what food we want it to have, or it trains us on what it wants to eat. If we don't train it, the flesh will eat any and every thing—whether it is healthy for us or not—and it will eat at any time it wants to.

If we want love, a misguided love, and sex, then the flesh will seek it out. If we don't train it, then it will find a distorted love wherever it can and have sex with whom and whenever it wants—no control. We cannot deny our flesh as it is a part of us, a part of our trinity: body, mind, and spirit. However, it must be in balance and trained to perform the tasks that we assign to it.

These tasks are the gifts that God has given to us, our calling and the purpose in our life.

In training our flesh, we must have parameters and specific goals in mind.

An example would be when we want to change something about ourselves or to obtain something in our lives.

The two most important things are;

1. Define the goals

2. Clarify the results

3. We accomplish this with these very simple little steps.

We set a time frame in which we want the desired result.

We then determine by what means we are going to receive; that is, what we are willing to do to get it.

The flesh then must go, get and deliver to us as instructed.

If we were to ask God what spiritual attacks we are under and want to stop or get rid of them, then we can pray for God to reveal to us what that spirit is. Sometimes it has several issues, many different things that we need to battle and have victory over. But God will reveal trials one at a time, the most important, at that moment, is what God will place on your heart. The Holy Spirit will guide you on how to deal and overcome it.

Once God has revealed to us what the spirit is, through revelation from the Holy Spirit, then we can proactively attack it and become victorious over it.

Let's say that I am under spiritual attack by the spirit of anger and aggression. This hinders me in my relationships with others. I end up hurting those that I love and care for, so I want to change this behavior.

The first part I need to do is to recognize that, that is what it is and not deny it. To see in my mind's eye where this behavior has had a negative impact, how the results of the behavior have affected myself, and the impact that it had on others, particularly those closest to me, the ones that I love the most.

I would go into prayer and fast. I would tell God that I recognize the attack and where it is coming from, ask His help in combating it, and state what I am willing to do to get the desired results.

Anger being the issue, the desired result would be a calmer, more understanding, patient, and a more caring person, sensitive to the needs and feelings of others. To have peace and joy in this life, to love and be loved.

When the spirit of anger approaches, you are quick to recognize the change in your behavior. One thing you can do is remove yourself from the situation before it escalates into something more intense. If you cannot do that, then you should stop and slow down your thinking, acknowledge that this situation is leading into what could be an anger-producing situation, then you should start to pray. You pray that God strengthen you, that he gives you those things that you want as the desired result, that you already are the possessor of those things—calm, peaceful, patient, understanding, sensitive, and caring. And you hold on to these thoughts and images in your mind.

Don't let the spirit of anger talk you out of resisting the desire to get angry, even if you feel justified and right about your position and that you feel you have the right to get angry. If you let the spirit of anger talk you out of your peace and understanding, you lose again. That is the very behavior you want to change. Count it all joy every time you must face these tests and trials. Each time and each one only make you stronger and that much closer to God. Know that you can't do it without him; give him praise and thanks with every little victory you win.

By constantly resisting the adversary, it will tire of messing with you and flee because it knows the results and the outcome will only magnify and glorify God. He doesn't want to do that, so he leaves you alone just so that God can't be glorified by something that he did.

You see, it's not about you. It's about Satan's rebellion and his battle with God.]He tries to get all those that he can by tempting us with our fleshly desires. Wanting to fight or having anger issues is certainly going into the flesh and is operating from there. It is not easy, and it takes training to do it and to make it a habit. So this is where fasting comes into play.

In order to receive this new behavior you will fast for a specific period of time The fast can consist of anything that denies your flesh of something that it wants and likes. You take it away for a period of time to show your flesh that it must submit to your will. Know your flesh will rebel against you because you are taking away something that it wants, but that will last for only a short while.

You may commit yourself to a particular action like getting up from bed an extra hour early for the next week, spend time in prayer, and journal your conversation with God. This is a form of fasting, especially if your flesh likes sleeping as late as it can.

You have faith that you can do whatever it is that you commit yourself to and proceed by doing it because you said you would. Speak it into existence; speak it as though it is.

Hebrews 11: 1 (KJV)

Now faith is the substance of things hoped for, the evidence of things not seen.

Faith is a commitment with a corresponding action. You must make a commitment and follow through with a corresponding action.

You might also take something else away such as watching TV. If after dinner you like to watch television, don't watch TV after dinner for a week. Find another activity to do in its place instead. Perhaps you're reading the Bible and while reading, read everything in the Bible about peace, joy, understanding, patience, caring for others, and about what other great men of God did, how they acted, and the results God bestowed upon them. and the results of those who didn't.

You read about the very subject that you're fasting on. You keep it in the forefront of your mind. Maybe go for a walk or a family talk, perhaps even start a family Bible study. This will add up to training the flesh to submit to your will. Once you have done the fast for the declared period of time, go treat your flesh to something that you know it enjoys, a form of reward for doing what you told it to do.

While you were fasting and waking up early and not watching TV, you were studying God's word, becoming closer to him, developing the ear to hear his voice and the vision to see his hand at work. That is why prayer and fasting go hand in hand. Fasting is the discipline that keeps the flesh in check so that it opens the doors to the spirit through prayer. Once in the spirit, you can communicate directly with Father God and have nothing blocking or getting in the way. Fasting is for the flesh as prayer is for the spirit.

Fasting is the tool we use to train the flesh. Once we have trained the flesh, then we can bypass the fleshly world through that thin veil that separates the two and enter the spiritual world without interference and with clarity. We can enter the spirit world with prayer as our ticket of passage. Once there, we can have a clear and defined purpose and a positive result to our prayers. We can use our flesh to bring to us that thing that our spirit has commanded, not the other way around. We have dominion over all creatures of this earth, and that includes our own selves, our own flesh. So I fast!

Fasting opens our hearts to recognize our emotional hurts and pains and helps provide a way to understand where they come from. Once we understand where they come from, we can deal with them better and overcome those issues for an enhanced and healthier, emotionally stable life.

Our emotions are the strongest part of our lives. We base decisions, actions, and reactions on them. How we may feel about things and our emotions are the easiest way for us to be misled and manipulated by those that are clever and persistent enough and have the desire to attack us that way. Get us emotionally involved and then they can sway us to their particular point of view. Love is an emotion, the strongest emotion of them all. Some might argue that hate is even stronger. Someone who is in control of their emotions is thought to be more reliable and dependable. We even speak of how well someone controls their emotions as a positive attribute, a good thing to say about them.

We even say "don't let your emotions get the best of you" to someone as a word of advice, knowing how dangerous our emotions can be. We also advise people not to make decisions in the heat of the moment, when their emotions are at a peak, and that the heat of passion has fueled those fires; we advise them to think things through when they have a chance to cool down or that the emotion at the moment doesn't get the best of them.

Murders are mostly considered an act of passion or emotional upset and the spirit of regret resides in, after the fact, and our lives are too full of regret. Our emotions can even have us declared legally as "temporarily insane."

Fasting helps us control our emotions better because it allows us to move into the spirit of God. We can ask God's understanding of an emotional situation through prayer, this then leads to wisdom. It helps us to have a clean heart, helps to know who and what to serve, our emotions or the Lord. It will help us to exchange our weak hearts for joy in our lives.

We fast to improve our physical health. When our bodies are attacked by illness and disease from anything like the common cold to cancer, we see that we are in better condition and prepared to fight off these attacks to our bodies. Fasting helps to promote the healing process of our bodies. It helps to control the chemical balance when we are out of it. Fasting along with a proper and healthy diet will prevent many illnesses in the renewing of our cells and cleansing of our blood. Oxygenating blood, converting foods into fuel so that for our bodies will function properly, the way God designed them to function.

By maintaining periodic and regular fasts, we can keep our bodies functioning at its highest capabilities. By maintaining a proper level of antioxidants, antibiotics, and vitamins and nutrients when the body is attacked, our bodies are better capable of fending off the attack. We are less susceptible and vulnerable to more serious complications.

So I fast! I fast for my health: my spiritual, emotional, and physical health.

Journal
The Second Hour
I Fast

_____

_____

_____

_____

_____

_____

_____

_____

_____

_____

_____

_____

_____

_____

_____

_____

_____

_____

_____

_____

_____

_____

AN INVITATION

By definition, the word "invitation," according to the Merriam-Webster's Collegiate Dictionary, is an action as in inviting. To get a clear understanding of what an invitation is, you need to look at the definition of the word.

1. To request the presence or participation of in a kindly or courteous way.

2. To request politely or formally

3. To act so as to bring on or render probable

4. To call forth or give occasion for

5. To attract, allure, entice or attempt

6. To give invitation, offer attractions or allurements

7. To entertain or offer shelter

God has given you an invitation to test Him and see the results for yourself.

"So that you might believe."

In a kind and courteous way, God is requesting your presence to participate with Him in this test.

God has invited you to get to know Him, to believe in Him and to have faith in Him.

To attract and allure you, He has promised you blessings and eternal life with Him in heaven. Not an empty promise of words and of no action, but a promise of life everlasting in paradise.

That you should lack for nothing in this life, that all areas of your life be fulfilled and rich, that you be blessed in your finance, your health, and your relationships.

God has offered an invitation to be tested in this matter.

According to the New King James Version, God has requested politely and formally:

Malachi 3:10-12 (KJV)

Bring ye all the tithes into the storehouse, that there may be meat in mine house, and prove me now herewith, saith the Lord of hosts, if I will not open you the windows of heaven, and pour you out a blessing, that there shall not be room enough to receive it. And I will rebuke the devourer for your sakes, and he shall not destroy the fruits of your ground; neither shall your vine cast her fruit before the time in the field, saith the Lord of hosts. And all nations shall call you blessed: for ye shall be a delightsome land, saith the Lord of hosts.

His attempt to entice you and to appeal to your sense of value and worth is in His promise. It is expressed by his words. "Then all the nations will call you blessed for your land will be such a delight."

This as an act on His part so as to bring on and render probable the foundation of your faith in Him and call forth His promise of abundance in your life, so you will learn to trust in Him for all your needs.

God has given an invitation for you to entertain, an offer of His shelter, His covering, His protection, and a partnership in a two-way relationship between the both of you, you and God together.

This perhaps is one of the most remarkable things God has ever done.

The creator of the entire universe, He who made all things and without Him nothing was made, He who knew your name before the earth was formed and time was created has given you an invitation to get to know Him personally. Follow His instructions and He will even let you test Him first if you would but just try these things His way and then find out for yourself.

He will bless you with more than you could possibly be able to store or keep, beyond your ability to imagine. He will bless you with more.

God even says "others will notice it and speak of it amongst themselves" of how blessed you will be.

Malachi 3:10-12 (KJV)

And all nations shall call you blessed: for ye shall be a delightsome land, saith the Lord of hosts.

God has given you an invitation!

God has offered an invitation; it is a gift for you to accept or reject. And the choice is yours. But because it is a gift, by what right can you choose to refuse it?

Everything God has done is by invitation. God's work is complete. He has done all he is going to do, it is written and it is so. So be it!

As for you, you need yet go through and live your life. You cannot see the future except through supernatural vision, and vision in the spiritual world will allow you to see that which is yet to come. He has given to you an invitation to be able to see the work in your life that he has already completed. If only you choose to accept his invitation.

If you accept God's invitation, he reveals to you the promise of salvation, the promise of an inheritance of everlasting life.

Jesus said, "If a man thirsts, let him drink from these waters, and he will never thirst again."

John 4:13-14 (KJV)

Jesus answered and said unto her, Whosoever drinketh of this water shall thirst again: But whosoever drinketh of the water that I shall give him shall never thirst; but the water that I shall give him shall be in him a well of water springing up into everlasting life.

Being the living water, he can make an invitation for you to accept or reject. He offers you an eternal relationship with him in paradise and that you will never thirst for anything again.

As He told one of the two thieves that hung upon the cross with Him the day He was crucified, one was complaining to Jesus.

Luke 23:37-45 (KJV)

And saying, If thou be the king of the Jews, save thyself.

And a superscription also was written over him in letters of Greek, and Latin, and Hebrew, This Is The King Of The Jews.

And one of the malefactors which were hanged railed on him, saying, If thou be Christ, save thyself and us. But the other answering rebuked him, saying, Dost not thou fear God, seeing thou art in the same condemnation? And we indeed justly; for we receive the due reward of our deeds: but this man hath done nothing amiss. And he said unto Jesus, Lord, remember me when thou comest into thy kingdom. And Jesus said unto him, Verily I say unto thee, Today shalt thou be with me in paradise.

It is as though he set this up this way on purpose, so you may be able to see the choice with your own eyes, even as he hung on that piece of wood. He hung on that piece of wood as though on purpose, so you may be able to see the choice with your own eyes.

From there, you have two choices.

One, you can mock and ridicule and not believe in Him and the results that will be. But where do you think that man is today? Where is it do you think he ended up when he came before Almighty God for his final judgment?

Or on the other hand, visualize this in your own mind, stop for a moment, and think; see it for what it really is. Why were there only three that day?

Nailed to a tree for all to see, Jesus in the middle, his arms outstretched, pointing to one thief to his left and one thief to his right.

When the Romans crucified people, they did it in bunch to make a point to the people of the price to be paid if they should resist them. The stark reality of the complete brutality for any that may defy them, the harshness and severity of their punishment for everyone to witness and give testimony.

Why on this day were there only three? Why two thieves? Why not a thief and a murderer or a rebel and a rapist?

But there were two thieves. What is it that a thief does?

They come to rob and steal. Is it not that what Satan does, to come to rob, steal, destroy, and kill?

Could Satan have had one of his own nailed on a tree right there next to Jesus? Continuously tempting Him even unto His last breathe and the very last moment of life; to give up His purpose—the shedding of His blood for our very redemption. Mocking Him and telling Him to call down the angels from heaven and deliver Him or for being the Son of God to save Himself.

Much like he did when Jesus first had been baptized, in the Holy Spirit by John the Baptist, in the River Jordan; went out to the wilderness for forty days and forty nights to battle temptation.

Lucifer told Him to throw Himself off the cliff and have the angels catch Him.

Matthew 4:2-6 (KJV)

And when he had fasted forty days and forty nights, he was afterward an hungred. And when the tempter came to him, he said, If thou be the Son of God, command that these stones be made bread. But he answered and said, It is written, Man shall not live by bread alone, but by every word that proceedeth out of the mouth of God. Then the devil taketh him up into the holy city, and setteth him on a pinnacle of the temple, And saith unto him, If thou be the Son of God, cast thyself down: for it is written, He shall give his angels charge concerning thee: and in their hands they shall bear thee up, lest at any time thou dash thy foot against a stone.

Jesus said, "Thou shall not tempt the Lord your God!"

Jesus did not submit to the devil's temptations that day either.

The focus of the world was brought to one point for that key moment.

It was either one or the other.

There were no other choices, no distractions, nothing else to get in the way. It was made so that we could see exactly what was at stake. Make no mistake about it!

Jesus might have said "to my left, you can have this" as your eyes follow his outstretched hand, and there nailed to another piece of wood is the ridiculer, the mocker. with birds landing upon his head and plucking out his eyes, being tormented and completely helpless to do anything about it; and to the Jews being nailed to a tree was a symbol of a curse.

Then Jesus might have said "to my right you can have this" as his arms are nailed to the cross, symbolically saying through him, you can break this curse.

Again your eyes follow his outstretched hand to the second man; the man that acknowledged him before others, publicly proclaiming him as the Messiah and rebuking the first by saying that they deserve what was happening to them. He wanted to be forgiven for his sins and to be remembered by Jesus when he goes into the kingdom of heaven before his father, covered in glory.

This convicted thief is allowing Jesus to stand in his place for the judgment that is to be handed down by the Almighty God, It is a just and fair God that allows us to make our choice. It is in His invitation and promise to us that our freedom of choice is found and also the consequences of that choice.

Can you see it? Can you see past the shallow surface of what appears to be the obvious, can you see to a deeper level of understanding to what really happened that day, even to Jesus's last breath?

He has also handed the options before you. If you do not accept His invitation, then that is an eternity separated from Him It is your choice.

Where do you think the second man is today?

Jesus is there with his arms wide-open, saying, "I love you this much!"

You have the same choice to make as these two men.

When you relate to one or the other and identify yourself with them, which one of the two are you? Which one is more like you and the one that you would like to be if you had a choice?

God does not force us to accept any invitation or gifts from Him. He is a gentleman and will not force Himself upon us. Jesus says,

Revelation 3:20 (KJV)

Behold, I stand at the door, and knock: if any man hear my voice, and open the door, I will come in to him, and will sup with him, and he with me.

If invited in, He will enter and dwell within you forever.

He is quite clear on the results of our choices, and He uses the Holy Bible to illustrate the results of these choices by using the examples of many different people and the choices that they had made.

The Holy Bible is not a book about Moses and Abraham; it's not a bunch of stories about David and Goliath or ancient Egypt. It truly is about the examples of God's behavior and His love for us and the instructions He] has given on how to make life this a heaven on earth.

It is the truth of Christ Jesus and the sacrifice He made, taking onto Himself the sin that would keep us from the presence of God. For every healing He performed, that illness had to go someplace else. For every demon He casted out, that demon had to go someplace else. For every iniquity He removed, it had to go someplace else.

As to where they went, they went back upon Him so that we do not have to suffer them.

Isaiah 53:5 (KJV)

But he was wounded for our transgressions, he was bruised for our iniquities: the chastisement of our peace was upon him; and with his stripes we are healed.

By your choice, do you stand before God at the final judgment, to accept the payment for your actions and thoughts? Or do you have someone to accept the punishment for sin in your place?

It has been proven, even in the spirit world, that for every action, there is an equal and opposite reaction. Or in other words, what you send out will return back to you.

It is an invitation to get to know God, to get to know who he is and how he acts, what it is that he wants for and from you and how to do it. He merely uses others to illustrate his point, the results of their choices and what you can expect when you come up against similar choices. God has given you an invitation!

Will you accept it?

Journal
The Third Hour
The Invitation

A PROMISE

A promise is a declaration of something that will or will not be done or given. An indication of future excellence or achievement, a pledge or an undertaking, to engage or join into, to assure and used in emphatic declaration, to afford ground for expectation.

This word of promise carries in itself a vision of hope, a commitment to believe. It is something that can be done for you or for others, knowing that within a certain time, something will end and something else will begin. That a change is going to come.

It is a word spoken that when heard, raises the heartbeat, quickens the breath, and widens the eyes. It extends a hand and puts a smile on your face. I promise it does!

When you were young, you were told by your elders not to make a promise that you cannot keep. By doing so, you are giving your word, and your word is your bond. It is a measure of your character; otherwise, you are made out to be a liar and cannot be trusted. There is much weight in this word of a promise and great responsibility that accompanies it.

God says that it is better to not make a promise, a commitment, or a covenant with him than to make one and not keep it; that really applies to anyone. You will be held accountable for the promises that you make; as it is said, so it shall be. Making a promise is the most serious and important thing you can do and should not to be taken lightly. A promise will determine your course of actions and be used as a measure of your expectations of those to whom have promised you. What will one do to make sure that they keep theirs once given, and what do you expect from those that promise you?

God has made you a promise!

We hold him accountable for his word and promise to us as he holds us accountable for ours to him.

There is strength and tenderness of understanding in it that when heard, it soothes and comforts. It brings joy where there is sorrow. It warms when it is cold. It feeds when there is hunger. It provides when there is lack. It consoles when there is heartache. It gives light where there is darkness. It restores that which was lost or stolen. It fixes that which is broken, and it heals when there is disease. It provides protection when under attack.

God gives promise in His Word. He gives promise to all that will just believe on Him. God gives the promise of everlasting life, redemption for sin, and to become a new creature through forgiveness, second and third chances; repentance and transformation.

Everything God has ever done has a promise attached to it. The promise can be a blessing or a curse depending on how one lives their life.

He promises reward, blessings, and abundance in this life, provided that we live it a certain way—by His laws.

He also promises the results of living life without Him and not obeying His laws, and that is a life that is cursed. The consequences of our actions and decisions are the things that become cursed or blessed. There always is a price to be paid for everything we do; the price can be a blessing or a curse. It can be more than we are willing to pay or more than we deserve to receive. But pay we will, every last cent of that which is owed and we will not be released from it until it is paid in full.

There is mercy and grace that we live under. And that is a promise God gave to us just as He promised the world that He would not destroy it as He did with Noah, and the reminder of that promise is in a rainbow!

The laws of God are applied equally to the just and the unjust alike. For each breathes the same air, bleeds the same blood, and receives nourishment from the same sun.

The results of a person's character are locked in their heart, and it can be seen through that person's actions. What is in the heart must come out; the true nature of a thing will always come to reveal itself in time.

The promise of God is never ending, and it never changes. It is the same always—yesterday, today, and forever. That is why we can trust it and have faith in it!

With the promise of keeping God's word and developing a relationship with Him brings the promise of blessings more than you could imagine or hope for, more than you could possibly store up.

The promise of not keeping covenant with God is eternal separation from him. If you choose not to have a relationship with him, your promise is to take responsibility for your actions yourself, and you will receive your just reward for those actions and those choices.

God is very matter-of-fact about these things. It is either one or the other, and that is it. It is that simple. No gray areas, no confusion, no "What ifs," and no buts. He is not a respecter of persons. He is a respecter of his law; He does know each man's heart and because of that comes mercy and grace, which may follow you all the days of your life. But His law, above all else, will be the final issue that any of you must deal with.

He has made a promise to all, and that promise came in the form of Jesus Christ, the promise that anyone who would believe in Him shall not perish but have everlasting life. Through Him came the promise of forgiveness for our sins. There is redemption, reconciliation with God, and hope that there is a life after this life on earth. The promise made to Abraham and his seed, to be the inheritors of salvation, and kept by the coming of Jesus.

In order to know how to have the peace and joy of His promise and live a life of delight and fulfillment, one must realize that there are other promises that God has made to you. And that is your purpose in life, to know and understand what that purpose is.

To walk in it is the key to your happiness.

How do you know what that purpose is?

It is simple. "If it won't let go of you, don't you let go of it!"

God has placed in us something that is unique, something that we really like. And when we are doing it, it's because we want to, and we enjoy it. Ever since we were born, this thing has been in us.

As we grow older, this love may seem childish. Then we are told to put childish things away and that these things are immature and irresponsible.

To make something out of our life, we are told that we must sacrifice our childhood dreams for work, never being taught that our childhood dream is our work.

How do we know what that is?

We know because it will never leave us. "If it doesn't let go of you, then don't you let go of it!"

We must figure a way to bring it to fruition for it to be a blessing to others as our gift is not so much for us as it is to be a blessing for others.

It also glorifies God, and you get enjoyment from doing it. It is something that you would do for fun and never the idea that you could be paid—and paid handsomely—would cross your mind.

What is in you that you love and brings joy to your heart, makes you feel that this is what makes it all worthwhile, be a blessing to others and can glorify God? Something that brings sustenance to others and with it, there is enough leftover to be of provision for you.

When you look at it this way, you find the key to understanding God's law of purpose and provision. It is not a matter of "when you get enough, you will give to others" but more a matter of "when you give to others, there is enough left to fill your needs" pressed down, shaken together, and running over.

For some, they have made it their hobby, not seeing it all the way through; Others have just a wish that they could have and never do.

A wise man once asked three questions and said that when you can answer these three questions—and the answers are all in line and are in conjunction with each other and can be applied to each question—then you will know the gift and the calling that God has put on your life, your purpose.

You then must learn how to cultivate it, to polish it, to hone it, and develop it into its fullest potential. This becomes your work, your labor, and God tells you to rejoice in your labor for it is a gift.

God's promise is when you can do this, your life will have purpose and meaning. And with purpose and meaning come joy and a sense of worth. You will feel that you have value.

How many lives are destroyed because people feel they have no value, that they have no worth, and that there is nothing to live for, no purpose?

People go to college, study for four years or more to obtain a degree, if they are lucky. Some never get to go to college or even finish high school.

Once these people have received their degrees, most don't even work in the field in which they have earned their degree. Are you one of them or know someone who is?

Is it any wonder why people are glad to see Friday come and regret that Monday is only two days away? It should be the other way round. Being glad that Monday has come, and Friday arrives too quickly, what a concept! Who in their right mind would even think such a thing?

And that is exactly the point, only somebody in their right mind would think of such a thing. Those that do not think this way have lost their right mind. Just like in the story of Peter Pan when one of the lost boys said he had lost his marbles. When telling others of Tinker Bell and his experiences, he came to find out years later that it really was only marbles.

Don't be deceived by the great lie that which is politically correct to say and popular with the masses. Don't let them rob you of your joy because most people have no clue on what it is they are saying. They only say things out of ease of conversation and habit, all the while keeping them from fulfilling the purpose that God has called them for.

Ask any person that has achieved great things in life, and they will tell you part of the secret to their success is that they love doing what it is that they are doing and that they would do it whether they were being paid to do it or not, that someone else is benefiting from it, but it is nice to make that kind of money for doing it.

Those that have lost their minds are easy to detect; they are easy to see and hear. They have problems on their jobs with their coworkers and their bosses, feeling unappreciated and underpaid. They complain all the time about everything and usually think that they could do better than the others. They are never satisfied with anything and seem to find fault with everything, never taking responsibility for something. They look for that "get rich quick" scheme or spend the weekend partying, abusing alcohol or drugs, even abusing their families—wives to husbands, husbands to wives and children, even themselves. It is because they have no purpose, no direction, and no satisfaction—nothing that "escaping for a while" can't cure, or so they think!

The problem is that it is always "only for a while" and "only for a while" always never lasts. It never can fill that void from walking outside of God's purpose.

The three questions that were asked by the wise man are:

1. If you were to be considered an expert on something, one of the world's foremost experts, and the world needed your opinion and were to be interviewed by the media, on what subject would they need to hear what you had to say?

2. If your next paycheck was the largest you had ever received but the smallest that you would ever get—after being paid for something that you would do for free just because you enjoy it so much that it shocks you that people would actually pay you that kind of money to do it, you would have to pinch yourself to make sure that you weren't dreaming—what is it that you did to earn that money?

3. If lying upon your deathbed, taking your last breath of life, having never retired from work, what is it that you did with your life?

"When you can answer these three questions," the wise man said, "and they all are in conjunction with one and the other, that one answer can fill each question. Then you know what your gifting is and your purpose in life."

When it is a blessing to others, and you enjoy doing it, and they get more out of it then you do, then you know that it is something that has been with you all your life. No matter how small or large it may be, do it!

If it doesn't let go of you, then don't you let go of it!

When we cast all our cares on the throne of grace and ask God to reveal to us through the Holy Spirit that dwells within us, He shows us.

According to Proverbs 16:9 (KJV)

A man's heart deviseth his way: but the Lord directeth his steps.

To truly know God's promise for you in life is to know your purpose, and you can only know that and how to do it when knowing him. How can you know who you are if you don't know who God is? That your heart is a heart after his own heart—not before his or instead of his, but after. When this is the case, he gives you your heart's desires. Then all these things shall be added unto you.

Knowing God's promise is to know that he has made a declaration of something that will or will not be done or given.

He has given you an indication of future excellence or achievement; he has made a pledge of an undertaking. He has engaged or joined in with you to become a partner with you. He used an emphatic declaration to afford grounds for great expectations, a vision of hope, and a commitment to believe. He has assured you that it is done for you and others, knowing that within a certain time, something will end and something else will begin.

It is in the power of the spoken word.

God has made you a promise, and He never goes back on His promises; otherwise, He would be made out to be a liar. God does not lie; otherwise, He would not be God!

God has made you a promise. He has given you His word, and His promise is in His word. Will you accept it?

His word has the power to manifest itself.

Journal
The Fourth Hour
The Promise

PLANTING SEED

God's Word

Seeds are the part of the plant that produces new plants, the embryo. It is symbolic of descendants or the hope of future growth.

The planting of seed, the laws of reaping and sowing, the laws of nature apply to the spirit world, as well as the physical world. They are the universal truths that our lives are governed by. There is no denying them; there is either knowing them and working within them or ignoring them either by ignorance or choice, thereby being subject to them. These laws have an effect, and they impact your life whether you believe in them or not. You can choose to learn them and how they operate so that you are in a position of ruling over them and having dominion as Jesus did. They will obey your word, all the elements of the earth and heaven, they will work for you.

Jesus positioned himself by knowing and speaking the Word of God.

Jesus knew that the words God had given him were full of life; and as he spoke them, they would produce the fruit of that seed and fulfill the purpose that God had intended. Everywhere Jesus encountered the enemy, Satan. He confronted him with the word of God. He was sent to destroy the works of the devil, and he did it by knowing and speaking the word of God. He did it aggressively and with certainty, knowing that the seed of His words reap the harvest that He planted. The power of speaking the word of God enabled Jesus to enter the enemy's territory, face him head-on, and be victorious over him, destroying the strongholds that the enemy had held in and over us with the sheer force of His words.

When Jesus spoke, He did it with such strength and conviction, knowing God's word does not come back void. It has the power to fulfill itself. He was able to defeat him at every step, and we are victorious in our battles with the enemy through Christ Jesus by doing what it is that He Himself did: knowing the word of God, speaking the word of God, having faith in the word of God, and knowing it is the truth.

By resisting him and speaking the Word, Satan had to flee; demons fell in its wake; the elements of the earth obeyed; the winds and the seas became calm; the eyes of the blind were cleared to see; the ears of the deaf were opened to hear; and when Jesus spoke, the dead rose—all from the planting of the seed of the word of God in the fertile soil that is Jesus and the expectation of what the word promised, to bring forth the harvest of its purpose.

Jesus never begged or pleaded with the Father to heal. No, Jesus knew that it is the will of the Father to heal and prosper us and to give dominion over all things of this earth. He didn't pray for our healing; He commanded it through the promise of God's word. Jesus wasn't passive and soft with His words; He was aggressive and took control of the situation, speaking the word of God with authority.

He knew God had anointed Him, and He walked in His anointing. It gave Him the confidence. Therein lies the hope of the world, that if we do as Jesus did, say what Jesus said in right, standing with the Father, we too can do and have as He aid that we can.

He spoke the words that the Father gave Him to speak; He said He does not say His own words. He does not speak of Himself but speaks that which the Father had given to Him. He did not doubt or question the results or the outcome; He stood firmly on God's word. He relied and trusted that God's word would be fulfilled; He spoke it as though it was, and it became so.

With His words came all that God had purposed for us on this earth: eternal life, love, peace, happiness, and the power to bring them to pass.

If we can just discover the simplicity of this action and learn to apply it, then we too can be victorious in the purpose that God has called us to do. We can bear the fruit of the seed that God planted in us and bring in the harvest that blesses others, provides for our own needs, and glorifies God.

Or you can ignore them, deny that they exist, or pretend that they don't apply to you and that you are in control of all the elements and every aspect of your life by yourself. That your existence here is solely by chance or that you evolved from an ape,, from some sort of missing link. And the reason they call it a missing link is that it doesn't exist; it is missing, and what is missing is exactly what is taught by the word of God. Or you can believe that there is no greater purpose in life other than "whoever dies with the most toys wins."

This is why there are so many people who have no vision of who or what they are and take on what the world says about them; they are confused and lost.

With the laws of nature, you work for them or they work for you. They rule over you, and you are subject to them; or you rule over them, and they are subject to you.

These are the laws that God operates by; the very laws that he wants us to be governed with, to understand them and how they work, so that we have control over them and be free from those things that would hold us captive and have control or power over us in the spirit world, as well as the physical.

The word *seed* has many meanings. There are parables, analogies, and many different ways to impress the significance of it and its purpose. We see it used to illustrate a point of planting and a harvest, that seed produces fruit; and yet again, they are symbolic to the point of understanding that what you do will bring forth a result. There are actions; and for these actions, there are consequences.

I believe that Jesus is the seed to all things; He is the seed to the knowledge and understanding of what your purpose is on this earth and how to fulfill it. The gift, the seed, that God has given to everyone lies deep within; it is planted in holy ground. He teaches us how to cultivate it, so the fruit that you bring forth is a healthy fruit worthy of reproduction and a harvest.

And here lies one of the main differences between Christianity and other religious beliefs; most others teach that you can earn your way into heaven or by your good deeds. You can make atonement for previous mistakes, or even overcome the bad from other past lifetimes. It is called the law of karma, which says that what you do will come back to you.

In other words, that seed you plant will bring forth the fruit of that harvest, good or bad, and that you are subject to these natural and spiritual laws, that you get what you deserve. However, with Christ Jesus, the Father God has given us, his children, a redeemer that took on the sins of the world—our sins, each and every one of us—so that we don't have to. This comes from one place and one place only, and all you have to do is believe and have faith; it is called grace.

With grace comes mercy; they are twin sisters in the spirit, so much alike and so very different. Each having its personality, its own special purpose, and its own relationship measured out to us by the Father. And these are given to us freely, even when we don't deserve them, even when we have planted wrong seed and deserve to have a harvest of wrong befall us. God provided for us a sacrificial lamb, by which a door opens, a means in which the delivery of grace and mercy can be received; thereby nullifying the laws of karma and rendering it useless and untrue for the believer. If you choose not to believe in Jesus as the Christ, then you are subject to those laws and will reap what you sow. The believer is forgiven his sins and becomes a new creature in the eyes of God for Jesus has agreed to accept punishment on our behalf, the punishment that we deserve. The nonbeliever, however, agrees to accept the punishment for his deeds himself, a choice of not allowing Jesus to take their place but rather pay the price and suffer the consequences for their sins themselves.

This is the seed that matters, the seed of his word that is planted in the holy ground of your soul and in your heart, the seed that dwells within you, the Holy Spirit, the seed of faith and hope.

Jesus illustrates the seed of faith in his parable of the Mustard seed, likening heaven to a mustard seed, which a man took and planted in his field, saying that it is the smallest of all seeds, yet when it grows, it is the largest of garden plants and becomes a tree so that the birds of the air come and perch in its branches.

So it is with the seed God gave us as our gift and the purpose and calling he has in our lives. As small as it may be at first, it becomes the greatest thing in our lives. It covers all things in our lives, and it eventually grows from a vine into a rooted tree. Not only does it provide for us, its purpose is to be there to support others as a shelter, strength, protection and a provider. Your faith being displayed by your actions, the words that come out of your mouth, how you approach things, how you view them, and what you do about them—these are in the choices that you make every day.

There is peace, joy, and calmness that come over someone that already knows the outcome of a thing, whatever that might be.

If you had read a book, watched a sporting event, or seen a movie; and you were sitting down with someone that had not seen any of that before, their reactions would be completely different than yours. Their emotions may become more involved, the level of anxiety heightened, physiological changes that can be measured, as well as felt. But because you have already seen it, you know what to expect, when and how to expect it. You have a sense of security as to the outcome and the events leading up to it. You don't get overly excited about these things; you see them as complete, finished.

As Jesus said, "It is done."

The seed of faith is found in the word of God; the Word is the seed. It is the seed for all things in your life, and Jesus is referred to as the Word. John 1:1 in the New International Version says it like this:

> John 1:1-5 (KJV)
>
> In the beginning was the Word, and the Word was with God, and the Word was God. The same was in the beginning with God. All things were made by him; and without him was not any thing made that was made. In him was life; and the life was the light of men. And the light shineth in darkness; and the darkness comprehended it not.

Understanding this seed of faith brings you hope— hope in your yesterday, your today, and tomorrow. That your yesterday had a reason, your today lets you see it for what it was and prepare you for what is to come, the promise of something better, a purpose.

What Jesus taught and what He did are tied inseparably to who He is. John shows Jesus as fully human and fully God. Although Jesus took upon Himself full humanity and lived as a man, He never ceased to be the eternal God who has always existed. The word is planted in holy ground, the holy ground being that of the Holy Spirit that dwells within you. For greater is He that dwells within you than he that dwells in the world.

Once we understand this truth, then can understand. God has planted a seed in us that He has called forth for us to cultivate and bear fruit. These are the gifts that we have, the very purpose for why we are here. The gifts that are planted in us that we are charged with to bring to harvest are for our self-fulfillment and to be used to benefit and be a blessing to others and glorify God.

Know that the spoken word contains all the power and authority that is with Jesus. This is why we must be very careful with the words we speak and what comes out of our mouths. The Bible says to speak it as though it already is. Speak it into existence. What we say does have impact. What we talk about is what we become.

There is an old saying that says, "Sticks and stones may break my bones, but words will never hurt me." How far from the truth that really is. We learn this saying as children; but it is a lie told to us by Satan so that our guard will come down, thereby trying to take on the impression that our words hold little if any significance. Satan attacks us early in life so that we may grow up with this already a part of our everyday thinking. This then undermines our faith. He knows that if he can get us to doubt the power of words, that they don't really mean anything or that we don't have to take them that seriously, then we won't use Jesus' words to build our faith. If he can get us to that point, it weakens our faith to the end—we stop believing in miracles or that we can even be in control of our own circumstances—so that we give up hope. Jesus has told us that all we need do is ask, have faith, we are of no consequence to him with any power, a less than zero to him, no threat. But with faith, we become very dangerous to him. You know that the Word has power over him and with our faith, we can resist him. The Bible says that if we resist, he will flee from us.

If Satan cannot control us in our thinking and in our beliefs, then we can walk in our calling. The seed that God has planted in us will come to its fruition and a harvest will follow. The question is how do you know what your calling is, what your purpose is in life, how do you know what it is that God would have you do?

You can tell what it is because you are born with it. It is something that has always been in you. It may just be the most simple of things that comes to your mind, but it is because you like it and always have. You can tell what it is when it is something that just won't let go of you; it is something that you always have thought about, and it just doesn't go away.

Know this, if it doesn't let go of you, then you don't let go it. That is a gift, a seed, that God has planted in you.

You may not be walking in it right now because you think that it is too simple and that it is silly for you to think that way. You think, because of your upbringing, that things must be more complicated than that; it is too simple, it will never work. This is a trick and a lie of the enemy, Satan, to make you think that something little isn't worthy of your pursuit as a career option and that you must work harder than that in order to become successful.

The most successful people do what they do because they love what it is they do, and they would do it anyway. It's just an added bonus that they get paid the kind of money that they do for doing it.

I don't mean to imply that it is as easy as breathing; it does take a lot of work to bring in the harvest of the seed that is planted.

With a gift comes the responsibility of cultivating it, nurturing and furthering it.

To grow a seed into a harvest, a farmer will have to have a piece of soil where he will grow this seed; he will clear the land of any and all debris, weeds, stumps, rocks, boulders, and the like. He will condition the soil and plow it. Once all this prep work is done, he then puts the seed into the ground.

But he has already had the seed while he was doing all the prep work. He plants the seed, a very particular seed of which he expects to receive in the harvest. He doesn't just randomly plant a seed, not knowing what it is or knowing what he is going to get when the time comes to harvest.

During the growing season, he nurtures that seed as it takes root and develops into a seedling. As it grows and becomes bigger and stronger, he waters it, feeds into it, and keeps animals away, those animals that would feed off of it before in grows to maturity.

He doesn't just put it in the ground, walk away, and expect to reap a plentiful harvest when it is time and in season.

Once the seed has grown into the plant—the plant has been tended to, watched over, and cared for and then the plant bears its fruit—it is now time to reap the harvest. But this too is labor; he doesn't just stand there and wish for the fruit to go into the baskets, he must physically put forth the effort to pick it, and this may require special kinds of tools to assist in bringing in this harvest. Once the harvest has been done, then the farmer must take it to market. From this harvest, he has brought in enough to be a blessing to others and a sufficient amount leftover to supply his own needs. This then becomes a glory to God.

Your personal gift, the seed, is no different in bringing out the bounty of a harvest. You must recognize what seed you have and where you are going to plant it.

You must prepare yourself so that your gift is rooted in the good soil of your faith and believe that it will come up as what you planted it to be. You must nurture your gift, train yourself in it, learn how to use it, keep the animals away from it as it is growing in its developmental stages, and learn to use the special tools that you need to bring in the harvest of your gift. When you do, it will be a blessing to others, and there will be enough leftover to supply all of your needs. This is where it becomes glorifying to God.

I have used this analogy for the purpose of illustrating that the word of God is in fact all the seed that you need to find your purpose in life and how and what you need to do to make it come into existence. How you are then able to live a purpose-driven life to find peace and contentment in that which you do.

Again, I mean not to imply that it is all that easy to do. It is labor, but a labor of love, a fulfillment of that which it is in your heart. And when your heart is after God's own heart, he gives to you your heart's desire.

For those who think that you can get by just because you think about doing something and not put the energy into doing it and then say that God knows your heart. Well, all I have to say to you is this: Yes, it is true God does know your heart, but do you know his?

Albert Einstein was once asked, "Do you believe in God?"

He replied, "I do not believe that a great somebody has planned every day of my life. I do believe that He led me down the garden path!"

When asked: "Do you believe He created the garden?"

He answered, "I believe He is the garden!"

Journal
The Fifth Hour
Planting Seed

GROWING SEASON

Learning to Apply God's Word

The growing season of your life is met with certain promises and obstacles.

One of the first things you need to bring in a harvest is the seed that has been planted in you, hope!

In the King James Version of the Holy Bible, Hebrews 6:11–19 says,

And we desire that every one of you do shew the same diligence to the full assurance of hope unto the end: that ye be not slothful, but followers of them who through faith and patience inherit the promises. For when God made a promise to Abraham, because he could swear to no greater he sware by himself. Saying, Surely blessing I will bless thee, and multiplying I will multiply thee. And so, after he had patiently endured, he obtained the promise. For men verily swear by the greater: and an oath for confirmation to them and end of all strife. Wherein God, willing more abundantly to shew unto the heirs of promise the immutability of his counsel, confirm it by an oath. That by two immutable things, in which it is impossible for God to lie, we might have a strong consolation, who have fled for refuge to lay hold upon the hope set before us. Which Hope we have as an anchor of the soul, both sure and stedfast, and which entereth into that within the veil?

To realize the promise of a harvest through the seed that we have planted requires from us these things:

Diligence of hope to the end

Faith and Patience

Endurance

God's counsel

Hope anchors your soul, it is sure and steadfast. Without which, you will surely become adrift and miss the harvest and fruit of your purpose.

As you enter God's growing season, base your expectancy on the hope that is in you. As your hope grows, so does your expectations. You start to expect the seed that you plant to bring forth the fruit of that which you intended.

As you see it blossom and flower into the fruit of your purpose, you watch it as it grows, your level of expectation grows, as well does your hope and each in equal proportion one to the other. This allows you to give yourself permission; it gives you the right to expect the reaping of a harvest, to bring in the fruit of your labors.

The word hope, in the Random House Webster's College Dictionary is defined as:

The feeling that what is wanted can be had or that events will turn out well.

A person or thing in which expectations are centered.

To look forward to with reasonable confidence.

To believe, desire, or trust

To feel something that is desired may happen

To place trust; rely.

Hope is one of the three main pillars of Christian character; the others are faith and love. One translation refers to love as charity. It is an essential and fundamental part of the life of all Christians.

It must be cultivated and proven over time.

Jesus not only had hope in the words He said. He expected these words to do what He said do and bring forth that which He spoke.

In the book of Hebrews, Paul instructed the people to not be spiritually lazy about developing their hope; he instructed them to understand it, what it does and what it is. That by developing their hope, their faith and patience would also grow; their expectations of receiving God's promise would be fulfilled.

These are measures of the spiritual world, not of the physical world.

In the physical world, our expectations have been developed by what we see, hear, feel, and think—the use of all our physical senses.

I believe that God wants us to base these measures on our hope.

The use of our spiritual senses—our salvation, righteousness, faith, truth, peace, and the sword of the spirit, which is the word of God, and in it is hope.

That it is based on him, and the trust that his word is all the seed that we need to be fulfilled in his promise.

His word never changes; it never lies or misleads us. It is the same yesterday, today, and forever.

We are told that our battles are not of the flesh, the physical world, but rather against principalities and dominions, the spirit world. The only way to have victory over the spiritual world is through a spiritual battle, in which Jesus already has victory.

He knows how to defeat the enemy and has given us instructions on how we can do the same. We only need to follow his instructions and apply his techniques.

Jesus wants us to know that hope, faith, and love work together and are intertwined like the finest linen on master weaver's loom—the three strand cord woven together, which is not easily broken.

Know what the definition of hope is, know the definition of faith, and know the definition of love, how they are interwoven and blended together, overlapping strands of each other, tucked and tied together. Apply them spread over and covering every circumstance that may be laid in front of you on the table of your daily life, a spread that covers from end to end and from the top to the bottom, every blemish.

This is where endurance and patience comes into the equation; by applying them daily, they will grow daily.

The growing season of a person's life may come at any time in one's life. It isn't a matter of age; it is more a matter of the spiritual maturity and the wisdom of the ages.

These ten hours with God have taught me that discovering God's purpose in my life is a long process. I am not saying that with any kind of braggadocios. On the contrary, it is with somewhat a hesitant embarrassment that I reveal this.

But I have learned that when God speaks, I obey. I feel that He has told me to put myself aside and do as He has said, so I am.

For some, it may come easily, finding God's purpose in your life. For others, it takes somewhat longer. I am an example of the latter.

Either case, the point is that you find it.

For me, it came to recognizing that I was not able to do all things on my own and that I had failed and made a terrible mess of my life. I hurt many people, people that I loved, believing that I could never hurt them, at least not willingly or knowingly.

This is where the real problem had laid in wait. You don't think that you are willingly or knowingly hurting the ones that you love but you are by not walking in your purpose, by not allowing God to make the provision for you in it, knowing that God does not call the equipped. He equips the call.

By relying on our own understanding, we are doing exactly that, hurting those that we love, especially ourselves.

For others, it may never come at all. These are the ones that become very dangerous to us all.

This is the unhealthy ground that Satan uses to plant seeds from the spirit of discouragement. We give up your dreams to the spirit of doubt and eventually give up on ourselves] leading us into becoming a creature of faithlessness. We feel a sense of hopelessness; and where there is no hope, there is only ruin and darkness behind the thinly disguised hidden veil that is the separation between the holy ground of truth and the bottomless pit of lies.

When we give up, we become an open invitation and easy prey for the devourer; he will enter in and rob us of our very life.

We will suffer in our life, watch our love ones suffer because of the mistakes that we made.

Until there is nothing left, nothing to believe in.

The fruits of these spirits are the fruit of disharmony and chaos, despair and worthlessness. We look at ourselves through the eyes of a failure, and we ridicule ourselves. We have a very low self-esteem.

The spirit of envy and the spirit of bitterness consume us until we are so blinded by them. We no longer see truth as truth, and we take up residence in the state of denial.

There comes a point when we get so tired of all the misfortune, the missed opportunities, the anger and bitterness. We feel that we can't even enjoy someone else's success or miracle.

We feel that they are no more deserving than we are, and we secretly would like to see them fall so that we feel better about ourselves. Why should they prosper if I can't?

It's saying to ourselves "If I can't have it, then nobody else can have it either!"

We become consumed with the spirit of vindictiveness, the spirit of anger, and the spirit of rage take over our thinking, causing us to become blinded by our own failures.

If anybody else succeeds, we take it as a personal affront and wonder as to why not me.

And why couldn't me be any clearer?

Then we wonder why people describe us that way, when we don't see ourselves through the same eyes as they. We would never describe ourselves that way. How misunderstood we are.

By learning about our relationship with Jesus and what God has purposed for us all of these other things can be defeated just as Jesus defeated them, by knowing and speaking God's word.

God may have brought us through some very rough times just to prepare us or what it is that He has purposed for us, to make us ready and able to stand fast in your calling because it is going to require the faith, hope, and love we have built up.

For us to have gone through what we have was necessary to get we the strength we need to go through that which He has called us to do.

Without having gone through what we have, we would have never been able to make it where He is calling us to go.

God put us through an on-the-job training to get us where we needed to be. Rejoice! Thank Him for loving you, preserving you, and having faith in you!

For others, it comes easier to them. They learn faster; they get it the first time around and don't have to take the same lessons in life over and over again.

They learn from a blessing to see the reward of a blessing. They don't have to go through the cost of disobedience to find out the reward for it.

Some people aren't so thick-headed and stubborn; they learn the easy way.

They learn that following God's word is joy and peace all of its own. They find that they can watch the hand of God move just as He said it would.

They acknowledge Him when they see it. They praise Him when He moves in their lives. They thank Him for all that they have, and they find joy in giving to others.

They learn to celebrate and to share in someone else's prosperity and miracles, knowing theirs is only just around the next corner.

They have learned through diligence, endurance, patience, faith, hope, and love that they can trust Him!

We need to learn God's word and study it, meditate on it, roll it around in our minds, contemplate it, grow in it, speak in it, and develop the ear to hear His voice.

Like stones that rub up against each other, spinning in a kettle, they chip off the rough edges and polish each other.

By doing so, our rough edges are chipped off, and we become polished in His word.

We need to have a full, one-on-one relationship with Him, and He will reveal the gift, the seed that He has planted in we. Through the Holy Spirit, He will show us how to develop, cultivate, and nurture His gifts so that we can walk a purpose-driven life that can bring us joy and blessings according to His promise.

Learning to apply God's word must start at the beginning. We must know what God's word is if we are to apply it.

In order for us to learn God's word, we must make an investment of recourses, that being a commitment of time, energy, finance, and a means to do it.

We need to buy a Bible and read it, become members of a good, bible-based church that teaches the word of God line upon line and precept upon precept.

We need to fellowship with other Christian believers and become a part of the church and the ministry works that it offers. Be they large or small, we must participate and be willing to give our time and talents, our gifts.

We can become involved in small groups of restoration or helping the homeless, ministering over our children or becoming greeters—volunteering ourselves to serve. Mentor a group of youths by sharing our experiences with them and guide them in the ways Jesus has taught.

Over time, as we learn these things, it proves us faithful and God reveals himself in a more and more obvious way; we learn to look for and to Him in our everyday lives. As we learn the things that He reveals to us, we begin to apply them to our circumstances and our actions by what we say and how we say them, by what we do and how we do them.

Our outlook changes, our behavior changes, our lives change, our faith increases and our hope rises, our love starts to shine through like rays of sunshine breaking through the clouds as a sign of our strength, not as a sign of weakness.

Our confidence increases; we become bolder in our declarations, and we follow through with our words.

Our self-esteem rises, we feel better about ourselves; and we learn to forgive, not just others but ourselves as well.

Our understanding of that which we are in Christ Jesus becomes clearer and the Holy Spirit reveals to us those things that God has planned for us to do.

He rekindles old flames of our dreams and ambitions; He plants new seeds of giving to others and paying forward the blessings that we have received.

He opens doors of opportunity for us to step through; He offers us ways to fulfill ourselves in Him which in it and of itself is glory to God.

We learn that by waking up every day and giving Him thanks and avowing ourselves to Him gain by our prayers and choices, the angels in heaven rejoice and celebrate.

God finds us pleasing and bestows upon us His blessings, as it is His pleasure to bless us, to prosper us, and to restore us to Him.

He rejoices in us every time we acknowledge Him; it is in that and because we have exercised our freewill and chosen Him that God knows our heart; it is not an inward thought but rather an outward action.

Our hearts are shown by what it is that we do, not just what we think, not something that is hidden away from the eyes of others and kept just to ourselves in some deep private part of our minds with the illusion that only God and ourselves know what is there.

This is his glory and a firm statement smacked in the middle of Satan's face that we are more than conquerors through Christ Jesus and that he has no authority over us and no legal right to cause us any "dis-ease."

When we learn to apply God's word, we walk in the fullness of his promise. We bear the fruit of our harvest from the seeds that we have planted and this by discovering the seeds God has planted as our gifts and talents. By nurturing them, we earn the right to bring in that harvest.

Become rooted in a good bible-based church, study the Holy Scriptures, meditate on the Word, and act upon them by putting them to the test.

In Malachi 3:10–12, NIV, God spoke about testing him

> Malachi 3:10-12 (KJV)
>
> Bring ye all the tithes into the storehouse, that there may be meat in mine house, and prove me now herewith, saith the Lord of hosts, if I will not open you the windows of heaven, and pour you out a blessing, that there shall not be room enough to receive it. And I will rebuke the devourer for your sakes, and he shall not destroy the fruits of your ground; neither shall your vine cast her fruit before the time in the field, saith the Lord of hosts. And all nations shall call you blessed: for ye shall be a delightsome land, saith the Lord of hosts.

This us the opportunity and encourages you to test Him in a matter.

Do you think that He would offer us to test Him If He would fail the test?

Would you make such an offer if you knew that you would fail?

Once we have prayed, fasted, heard God speak, and offered an invitation, once He has made us a promise, and we start to plant the seeds of God's word in our life, nurturing the seed, and applying the word, we need to know that there will come against us many different tests and temptations.

Rejoice in them because God has strengthened you and has faith in you. He believes in the Holy Spirit that dwells within you.

Don't run and hide from these tests, know that you are now empowered to be victorious over them in Jesus name.

But know they are coming.

Journal
The Sixth Hour
Growing Season

TESTS AND TEMPTATIONS

Tending the Garden. Trusting God's Word

Seek with diligence and with passion the gift that has been planted inside of you. You have to want it and desire it; ask the Lord to reveal it to you in such a way that it is clear to you and have no doubt as to what it is.

Something you enjoy and feel good about inside. Something inside that makes you say to yourself, "I really love this, and it makes me feel good about myself."

Something that, as you learn more and more about it, your hunger increases; the appetite to learn all you can about it continues to grow. You thirst for more knowledge of it and are drinking from a bottomless well. Know that it is in Jesus that quenches this thirst, nothing else can!

Something that, while you are doing it, you can feel the spirit of the Lord working right beside you. You can see God's hand move; His spirit permeates everything about it, even in ways you would have never considered, and these ways are blessings to others.

Want it, need it, and desire it with all that you are. It is the air that you breathe.

Give yourself credit for being special enough, in his eyes, to be able to do it. Believe in yourself. Why not you? If not you, then who?

Believe in yourself as God believes in you!

If God says that you can, then who are you to say you can't?

Are you going to argue with Him about it?

Haven't you been doing that long enough?

You are special, and you do deserve this. You have the right to it; give yourself permission to have it.

It is the Holy Spirit that dwells inside of you that God knows and trusts.

Let Him guide you, He will give you the vision and the strength to do it.

When the Holy Spirit has revealed your purpose, and you have prepared yourself with the tools necessary to bring in the harvest of that gift, know there will be many times when you will be tested and tempted to let go of it as you walk in this path. You will be tempted to go back to where you were before you were awakened to it, still walking in a dazed and confused world you created by believing the lies of the one who hates you the most.

Take comfort in knowing that these tests and temptations wouldn't be coming against you if you weren't doing what God wanted you to do.

Ask yourself, why would the fallen one even care about me if you were not bowing to him anymore and giving your praise and worship to God instead of him?

Lucifer knows that if you walk in the purpose that God has given you, you become a danger to him.

So he tries to stop you in every way he can.

Now that you have been trained up in studying God's Word and using the methods that Jesus has taught, you can discern those things that come against you for what they are, lies and deceptions.

In the book of Nehemiah, God outlines specific ways in which Satan will try to destroy your work for the Lord and make you question your gift and the purpose that it has.

Recognize them because they come in the form of;

>ridicule and intimidation;
>
>threats of physical attack
>
>confusion
>
>discouragement
>
>the spirits of negativism;
>
>division among ourselves;
>
>temptation to compromise or reason with the world;
>
>exhaustion;
>
>fear;
>
>the leading of false prophets.

Satan's principalities and powers are highly organized; they hover above in the airwaves to come against individuals, families, cities, and nations.

Their purpose is to tear down all that is holy, all that is righteous, all that is pure, moral, and decent.

Their objective is to destroy families by turning husbands against wives, wives against husbands, and sow the seeds of rebellion within our children; this breaks down the community, then the cities and countries.

They will corrupt our leadership in government and in the church; it will cause them to compromise and negotiate with the terror that is spread in the virus that is fear as it blows in the winds of acceptance.

Our courts and legislators yield to these powers as to be nonconfrontational, bowing down to the politically correct thing at the time, sacrificing what is morally right by putting our necks on the chopping block of compromise and tolerance.

This then affects one person to the next, to the cities, the country, and the whole world.

Yea I say unto you, the same is true in reverse. We can take up and put on the full armor of God, become strengthened in our purpose, leading our families in the ways of God, committing to serve in our churches and communities.

If you were to hear negative comments—like that you are no good at what you do; what you are doing is a bad idea; it will never work; you'll have to get up too early, go to many places, speak to too many people, yet nobody will listen; and that you have no talent for the calling that you profess, but you know that it came from God—then you can be reassured that it is the devil trying to uproot you and prevent you from bringing in the fruit of the harvest God has intended for you in the valley of His delight, to harvest from the vineyards of truth the grapes of peace and joy.

If you are called to be a preacher, then preach.

If you are called to be a singer, then sing.

If you were called to play a musical instrument, then go buy one and practice, practice and practice some more. Practice until it is a part of you, and you are a part of it.

It's kind of like the old joke "How do you get to Carnegie Hall?"

The answer? "Practice, practice, and practice!"

Learn all you can about it, be a student of it. Know its history, and make it your future.

Become expert in it, and know that if it is something that God has planted in you, you will love to do it anyway.

Use the love you have for it as your motivation, and do it as unto the Lord.

Know that while you are perfecting it, there will be trials and errors. There will be frustrations and dead ends. Just let the Lord guide your steps; and in the morning, get up and do it again.

A guitar player may hit the wrong note, maybe bloody his fingers until he builds up calluses.

A mathematician may get a wrong equation, have a theory that doesn't prove.

A writer may misspell a word, have a writer's block.

An actor may forget his lines, miss a cue, and even have stage freight.

This is all part of the learning curve, until one day it all starts coming together.

It's not so much an effort to learn the secrets of your gift because now, it's more of the polishing of it.

It becomes so much a part of you that you cannot help but to do it; it is who you are, and it is what you do!

The Bible says that the righteous man may fall seven times, but he gets right back up again.

If we fall down, get back up again. Never stop serving the Lord. Apply the lessons you have learned while in training; ask for His guidance, His forgiveness, and He will restore you.

Remember to always give Him praise and thanks when things go well; remember your source as Jesus did.

Remember it's not what you go through but how you go through it.

This then becomes the resistance that the Bible speaks of, causing Satan to flee.

Whenever he rears his head and see you praising God and giving him glory, Satan cannot stand that; it is like fingernails scratching across a chalkboard to him, and he will flee.

He does not want to be your source and reason to be praising and glorifying God, so he leaves.

As your gifts grow, remember to put on the "full armor of God."

And know the Bible says "put on the full armor of God," but I can't find any verse where it says to take it off.

So to me that means you have it on always, through everything all the time.

The Bible says in Ephesians 6:10-20 (KJV)

Finally, my brethren, be strong in the Lord, and in the power of his might. Put on the whole armour of God, that ye may be able to stand against the wiles of the devil. For we wrestle not against flesh and blood, but against principalities, against powers, against the rulers of the darkness of this world, against spiritual wickedness in high places. Wherefore take unto you the whole armour of God, that ye may be able to withstand in the evil day, and having done all, to stand. Stand therefore, having your loins girt about with truth, and having on the breastplate of righteousness; And your feet shod with the preparation of the gospel of peace; Above all, taking the shield of faith, wherewith ye shall be able to quench all the fiery darts of the wicked. And take the helmet of salvation, and the sword of the Spirit, which is the word of God: Praying always with all prayer and supplication in the Spirit, and watching thereunto with all perseverance and supplication for all saints; And for me, that utterance may be given unto me, that I may open my mouth boldly, to make known the mystery of the gospel, For which I am an ambassador in bonds: that therein I may speak boldly, as I ought to speak.

Each piece of armor is symbolic; it has a special purpose and significant attributes, and they are there for a reason.

The girdle of truth completely wraps around you. Jesus is the way, the truth, and the life. Be completely wrapped in the truth, lies cannot get through to you.

The breastplate of righteousness protects your heart. We can be manipulated by our emotions and hard hearts and led into behaviors in the heat of the moment.

The preparation of the gospel of peace allows you to be ready to preach the Gospel to all ears; you are always ready to proclaim Jesus.

The shield of faith lets your faith be put out in front of you and keeps any and all lies or attacks against you at bay. You are unwavering, undaunted, rooted and steadfast; your hope lets you know the glory of God and realize his promise.

The helmet of salvation acknowledges Jesus as Savior, the author of salvation; it protects your ears, your mind, and your eyes. Your mind does not become confused; your ears don't hear the negative; your eyes sees clearly and is not be blinded by illusion.

The sword of the Spirit, the living word of God. Jesus is the living word. The sword of the Spirit is the spoken word of God, it is a double edge instrument used to defeat the enemy when you are under spiritual attack. Quote the word of God, that which is written in the Holy Bible, and that of Jesus as your example and champion to fight your battles on your behalf.

"In the beginning was the word and the word was with God and the word was God and the word was made flesh and dwelt among us."

By using God's word against all enemies, you are able to have victory over your adversary. Speak the word of God; it has the power to manifest itself.

Journal
The Seventh Hour
Tests and Temptations

The Eighth Hour

REAPING THE HARVEST

God's Blessing Is a Gift

According to the Apostle Paul in.

> Romans 11:29 (KJV)
>
> For the gifts and calling of God are without repentance

The word *gift* defines in the Merriam-Webster's Collegiate Dictionary as:

1. Something given voluntarily without payment in return, as to honor a person or an occasion or to provide assistance; present.

2. The act of giving.

3. Something bestowed or acquired without being sought or earned by the receiver.

4. A special ability or capacity: natural endowment; talent —*a gift for music*

5. To give some power, capacity, or talent to.

6. To present (someone) with a gift: *just the thing to gift the newlyweds.*

I use these words of harvest, *seed, fruit,* and *gifts,* as spiritual imagery so that we may better understand the concept of what a harvest is, how *seed, fruit,* and *gifts* are the same thing. Cultivating them is labor, and it requires time and actions to bring them into fruition. It is impossible to fulfill your God-given purpose unless you revere God and put Him first in your life. Because we have an eternal value, it is also impossible for us to be truly satisfied with the temporary things of this earth; there is nothing permanent to them. They grow and die because we were created in God's image. We were thought of before the foundations of the earth were formed. We can never be fully satisfied with the temporary pleasures of this life, only an eternal relationship in which God fully satisfies our needs.

God has voluntarily planted in the fertile ground, which is the Holy Spirit within us, a special ability, a seed. It does require a payment of sorts and that payment is learning what that gift is and how to use it, to cultivate it—nurture it until the seed matures and brings into existence the fruit it was intended when planted—then to harvest that fruit. Bring it out so that others have access to it, making it available so that God is glorified and others may be blessed by it.

In the using of our gift, the harvesting of the fruit, which the seed brings forth, is used to honor God and be a blessing to others; and then it is meant to be provision for you.

When we have learned what our gift is, we have nurtured it, which is our work. That is why God says that we should rejoice in our work for it is a blessing. Those who don't understand this are the very ones who need to learn what their gift is because they are not walking in it or doing what it is that God has called them to do. They are the ones who are frustrated at work or never seem to be fulfilled. They have no purpose, no joy.

Once you have started to grow in your gift, your relationship with God changes. It becomes a personal relationship; you have a clearer understanding of who you are and why you are here, the answer to the age old question "who am I and why am I here?"

When you have gone through the seasons of growing this seed into a fruit that you have harvested, once you have learned how to protect it from those things that would mean it harm you can enjoy the sweet nectar of your labor and rest in the glory of knowing you have done what God has asked of you. Like a farmer that puts up a scarecrow to keep those away that would do damage to his crop, you must also put up a scarecrow of your own in the garden of your spiritual gift, the seed that is planted in you. That scarecrow is the body of Christ; it's the church and the word of God that protects your seed. This will surely chase away any and all spirits that would come against it. When you have gone through the tests and the temptations, have tended the garden well, and have stewarded over the gift God has given you, then it is time to reap the harvest.

How do you know when it is time to reap the harvest?

You realize that your gift is different from anybody else. It is unique to you, and you cannot find yours in someone else. There may be others that share a similar gift, but each is measured out according to God's grace and need not be compared to someone else's gift, only that you use the gift God gave you by the faith that he has measured out to you. Use your gift to glorify God, not to pursue your own interests of self-glory.

It overcomes you, it takes up most of your thinking. You breathe it like you do air. You eat it like you do bread. You drink it like you do water. It becomes you and what you do. But when you drink of this water, like Jesus said about drinking from this well, you will never thirst again. Meaning, it quenches those things in your life that you have been searching for. It lets you know you have found it, your search is over. Now rejoice in your work.

You can now see things as they truly are, not as someone else has told you. You see them as though they are complete, as if they are already done.

Know you will always have to battle the forces that come against you; but now you have learned how to resist, and you know why they keep coming to attack you. It is because they don't want you to walk in the purpose that God has gifted you with. Satan and his minions will always fight against you until he learns that you call on God every time you are attacked and claim to God that Satan is the reason you stopped seeking God out in prayer because he was messing with you. Satan hates that; the last thing he wants is for you to go running to God because of something that he did. What he wants more is for you to run away from God because of something you think God did not do.

For example, not answering a prayer that you put before God or that he didn't show up in the midnight hour when you needed him to pull you through a situation. You should know that those things that are not answered by God the way you might have expected should tell you something. And it is that those were your expectations and had nothing to do with God.

It is both the consequence and the result of something that you did or didn't do, or it has to do with someone else's relationship to God and not yours. You are not responsible for them and their choices, they are!

By reaping the harvest God has blessed you with, you learn to count on him as your provider and protector and that all things work together for his glory. If you can see this, it takes the pressure of being responsible for all those other things off of you as he has control over all of it and wants you to not have to worry about those things.

The special ability, the natural endowment, the gift that God has bestowed upon you will become that glory to Him. That blessing to others and that provision to you, the inheritance and legacy to your children's children—these, the gift, will transcend this world's confines and limitations. It will deliver you into a place of power and authority that God has ordained for you, and it will give you dominion over your world and those things in it.

The how-to part comes from Jesus as he said,

> Matthew 6:33-34 (KJV)
>
> But seek ye first the kingdom of God, and his righteousness; and all these things shall be added unto you. Take therefore no thought for the morrow: for the morrow shall take thought for the things of itself. Sufficient unto the day is the evil thereof.

Let your heart be your guide and let God order your steps. Pray for His wisdom in following the lead of the Holy Spirit and know He is looking out for you in all you do. Even when you have to make adjustments in your plan and the direction you are following.

In proclaiming to God what it is that believe He has ordained as a purpose you to do, what that seed is that he He planted in Him out, that your soul is full of good and that it is not a work of vanity. For what profit is there in a man seeking the riches of gold and silver if God is not the center of it? As it written in the,

> Matthew 9:37-38 (KJV)
>
> Then saith he unto his disciples, The harvest truly is plenteous, but the labourers are few; Pray ye therefore the Lord of the harvest, that he will send forth labourers into his harvest.

Jesus tells us that not everyone acts upon the call of God in their lives."

Jesus also uses the parable of the seeds that are planted in a rocky place, in a thicket, and in good ground.

This parable tells us that some people's souls are likened unto a rocky place. Sometimes the seed will sprout, and a plant will grow but won't last long because there is no real root to sustain it. There are people like that, they flower for a moment, but they don't last.

There are those that spread their seed in a thicket. They may start to flower also, but they become choked by their surroundings, and they don't last. Then there are those that are planted in fertile ground. Their seed becomes rooted, it grows, it lasts, and it produces fruit.

Make sure that you till the soil of your soul with the spirit of God, and it will bring you life. Guard your thoughts and emotions so that the flesh does not rule over your spirit; this would be rocky ground and death, the seed will surely die. Watch out for the thickets of personal associations and old familiar habits, this will cater to the flesh and will also lead to the seed dying. Be sure that the seed God has given you is planted in fertile soil, the soil of the spirit of God, and it will grow and bring with it life and in abundance.

Journal
The Eighth Hour
The Harvest

The Ninth Hour

GOD FORGIVES

As we are all called by God to fulfill a purpose that He has ordained for us in our lives, some people never learned how to walk in their purpose, or they gave up on it. They just opened their hands and let it go as a wisp in the wind, always regretting, not living up to their potential, knowing deep down in their spirit that they are really better than that.

Some hear the call and answer it, only to let it slip away, merely to be left standing out in the cold of their gift and the fullness of God's promise, simply wondering what happened.

They are distracted from the task at hand and question whether it is really what they should be doing with their lives, their profession or avocation. They're left in the abyss of doubt and double-mindedness, living in the state of confusion at the intersection of unknowing and unbelief with the heartache of their own despair. They're left unfulfilled, living a life of regret, of emptiness, and sorrow.

You should know that we all make mistakes, and we all fall down; but the righteous may fall seven times, yet they get back up again. The key here is to *get back up again*.

Hopefully you don't keep falling in the same place; you may fall again with the aim of making it a little further than you did the last time. But keep getting up at each new turn or challenge, progressing each time. Like any good carpenter, eventually you learn to measure twice and cut once.

When we try and fail, we don't give up; we try again and again if necessary. We continually try until we finally make it. Diligent in our pursuit of a purpose-driven life, determined, persistent, and single-minded like the undaunted worker bee gathering honey.

This is where forgiveness, mercy, and grace dwell.

We must forgive ourselves for not being perfect; however, the forgiveness is not so much as forgiveness towards others, although the forgiveness of others is necessary for us to be able to receive forgiveness from the Father. By forgiving ourselves, it sets us free of the bondage the spirit of failure would hold over our heads and the personal attacks of Satan, who would have us question ourselves as to whether we are worthy or not, causing us to also do battle with the spirits of doubt and confusion. These are spiritual battles, not of the flesh; they require wearing the full armor of God and never removing it.

Enlightenment and forgiveness comes from knowing, and knowing comes from the word of God. God says that you are worthy, and you do deserve the fullness of He promises and his blessings; thus, Satan is a liar!

Give yourself permission to be all God has called you to be. You have been forgiven!

God must forgive us because He said He would, otherwise He would be made out to be a liar, and God cannot lie.

God said He would forgive us if we would confess and repent. God cannot hold a grudge against us once He has given His word. Once forgiven, it is as though our offense never occurred, wiped clean in the archaic records of heaven and covered by the precious blood of Jesus that he shed so that we might be forgiven.

How can God be in heaven with the intention of holding a grudge against us, yet He sent Jesus to stand in our place for the atonement of sin?

He can't!

Paul the apostle was forgiven and went on to write two-thirds of the New Testament.

He established new churches and spread the word of Jesus Christ as the Messiah everywhere he went, and that was his purpose.

It wasn't easy for this man to have accomplished what he did; he was able to do it through faith and perseverance, and it became his strength.

If this man can be forgiven for what he had done, so can we !

He had a personal encounter with Jesus and recognized it for what it was. From that, he went on to do great works in the name of Jesus.

Paul met Jesus on the road to Damascus, where he had a personal encounter.

You need a personal encounter with Jesus to help you walk in the purpose God has called for you.

I ask, have you had a personal encounter and dismissed it as a figment of your imagination or some other spiritual anomaly?

In God's forgiveness, we find our purpose; and in most occasions, it comes with a confirmation from a third party, not something that you would have to solicit. It comes to them in a vision or in a prophetic word. This is also a process. First, there is a personal encounter; there will be acknowledgement on your part that you have sinned and an asking for forgiveness, then there will be witnesses to the genuineness of the change that you have gone through. There is revelation to you through the Holy Spirit as to what your purpose or calling is. There will be a confirmation, so you must be obedient to it. It also requires study and time dedicated to learning all you can about what it is you are called to do.

Paul, once he had his personal encounter, went off for three years to study and learn of that which he was called for before he went out to do what he was gifted in, that being to preach the gospel of Jesus Christ, his message of salvation to the gentiles while establishing churches throughout the world.

The story of Paul and his personal encounter with Jesus on the road to Damascus as found in the book of Acts chapter nine of the Holy Bible. Before he was known as Paul, he was called Saul of Tarsus. He was well-known for hunting down and persecuting the new Christians, the Hebrew followers of Jesus.

He was known as someone who would kill them where he found them. His name was later changed to Paul.

Saul was commissioned by the high priest to go to Damascus with letters to the synagogues that any found to be worshipping Jesus, be they women or children, were to be bound and brought to Jerusalem. This could mean a death sentence to them, and they feared him.

As he journeyed and came near Damascus, a light fell upon him and shined around about him where he fell from his horse to the ground, and a voice was heard saying, "Saul why do you persecute me?" Saul answered, "Who are you?"

The voice then said, "I am Jesus whom you persecute."

There were other men who accompanied Saul and heard the voice but saw no one.

Saul lost his vision and could not see; the men who were with him picked him up and took him to Damascus.

There was also a disciple in Damascus by the name of Ananias, who in a vision saw an angel of God telling him of Saul. That he was to seek Saul out and lay his hands upon him to restore his vision. Ananias mildly protested because of Saul's reputation but was obedient to the word given him by the angel.

This was his personal encounter with Jesus; the others that were with him were witnesses. The revelation was that Jesus had risen from the dead and had called him to a purpose. Confirmation came from the vision that was given to Ananias; Paul's obedience was in going away for three years, studying and learning. Paul made himself ready for the things that he would be coming up against; it strengthened him and his faith.

Though Ananias feared Saul, he went to where Saul was staying and did as the angel commanded. Once he prayed and laid hands on Saul, Saul's sight returned to him. Saul repented for his sin, asked for God's forgiveness, and asked what it was that Jesus wanted from him.

It is then that God revealed to Saul what it was that he had purposed for him.

From this encounter, Ananias became a companion to Saul and mentored over him. He was a person the others in the community knew and respected.

This is how God operates; it is through His forgiveness that we will have a personal encounter with Jesus. There are those that will witness and testify to the encounter. He will place someone else in position to confirm, someone who is obedient to follow God's direction and reveal his purpose in your life. Have someone to minister over you, and he will transform you.

When those in Jerusalem that commissioned Saul heard of the change in Saul, they set in place a plan to have him killed.

But God will protect you from those who would mean to cause you harm and keep you from fulfilling your purpose, as long as you walk under his authority and obey his commandments.

When you do, all things that happen to you are used to glorify His name.

If we have had a calling that for one reason or another went unfulfilled—we might have succumbed to the pressures and the attacks of the enemy or have abused that gift ourselves—it is not too late to pick it back up and do it again. It only requires forgiveness, and forgiveness comes by asking. In asking, one must recognize what it is that we need forgiveness from; repent from it, and repenting means that we don't do it any longer, you have set it aside, it must be released to God and replaced with what it is God would have us do. It is only too late when we go before God in judgment.

Saul, who was now called Paul, went on to establish many churches and wrote, in essence, two-thirds of today's New Testament.

It is through God's forgiveness, a personal encounter, witnesses, revelation, conformation, repentance, and obedience that all these things are made possible.

Not only does Jesus have for us a personal encounter with others standing there as witnesses, He will also make for a personal encounter when we are alone and by ourselves with no one else around.

However, there will always be witnesses to the change in you. There will always be confirmation. There will be revelation to a purpose. It will always take obedience to the call or the gift planted inside of you, and it requires asking for forgiveness and repenting.

In the book of Acts chapter eleven, the Holy Bible tells of a personal encounter the Lord had with Simon Peter while he was in the city of Joppa. Peter was staying with a gentile by the name of Simon. Most of the new Christian believers felt that gentiles were unclean, and even referred to them as dogs. They thought that God had promised salvation to only them, while gentiles were here on earth only to pave the way to damnation.

Peter was one man that initially felt the same way. It was in the law that the Hebrews were not even to associate with gentiles, and for Peter to be staying with one was a very big deal for he himself had racial bigotry. But God was dealing with him on his prejudices that is why God had sent Peter there in the first place. While Peter was staying with Simon and while those of Simon's household were preparing a meal, Peter went to the pray at the housetop, where he fell into a trance. He was very hungry when he went up to pray, and he wanted to eat. While in the trance, he saw heaven open to him and a great sheet held by the four corners fell down around him.

In the vision, he saw four-footed beasts of the earth, wild beasts, creeping things, and the foul of the air. A voice said to Peter, "Arise, slay, and eat."

Peter said after hearing the voice, "No, I have had nothing unclean enter my mouth."

It was the tradition of the Hebrews not to eat these kinds of foods as by the Law of Moses. So for Peter to be eating these foods and with a gentile was a very big deal for those who were circumcised, meaning the opposite of his culture.

A second time, Peter responded to the voice in the vision; and again, the voice answered him saying what God has cleansed, call not unclean or common. This was done three times, then they were drawn back up to heaven.

Now at this time, three men entered into where Peter was staying, saying they had been sent there by the Spirit. These men were also gentiles sent by their commander, a Roman centurion who also had a vision and a visit from an angel. Cornelius, the centurion, was told by the angel where they could find Peter and to send men to seek him out.

These things are significant for several reasons. First, it shows God revealed Himself to a gentile, who by the way was obedient to the revelation given to him, proving God was a God for all, not just the God of the Hebrews.

Second, He also gave a vision and a visitation to Peter at the same time. God showed that He will reveal Himself to us while we are alone and not necessarily with others around at the time, but there is always confirmation to the vision.

Peter having to deal with certain prejudices he held needed to learn that God is a God for all people; and the very purpose for Jesus coming to earth. It was in preparation for the ministry Peter was called to, preaching the Gospel to the gentiles. God removed him from his comfort zone to teach and prepare him for his calling, and he will do the same to you.

God also showed that tradition was something not to be put above Him and what He has given us Peter's revelation was something more than him, the calling, the purpose, the seed; the gift God gave Peter was more than just he himself. It was something he couldn't do by himself; it was something that he could only do by relying on God as his strength and source. It was something he could not do alone; the others who were there were the witnesses and the confirmation to the vision for both Cornelius and Peter, as well as for themselves.

In this piece of history, God shows the same examples of his gifting and the activities that go along with it.

The personal encounter; the witnesses; the revelation; the confirmation; asking for forgiveness; repenting; and the separation from the comfort zone, moved to a place where you can grow in the gift, then be released to go forth and walk in it to bring in the fruit of the harvest—it all comes from God's forgiveness.

The only time it is too late to receive God's forgiveness is after you die.

Journal
The Ninth Hour
God Forgives

The Tenth Hour

GOD RESTORES

When they had landed, they saw a fire of burning coals there with fish on it, and some bread. Jesus said to them, "Bring some of the fish you have just caught."

Simon Peter climbed aboard and dragged the net ashore. It was full of large fish, 153, but even with so many the net was not torn. Jesus said to them, "Come and have breakfast."

None of the disciples questioned who this man was, they already knew He had been crucified, conquered death, and resurrected to life, proving He is in fact the one and only living Son of God. God himself, through whom we receive eternal life, manifests on this earth.

This can be found in the Holy Bible,

John 21:9-19 (KJV)

As soon then as they were come to land, they saw a fire of coals there, and fish laid thereon, and bread. Jesus saith unto them, Bring of the fish which ye have now caught. Simon Peter went up, and drew the net to land full of great fishes, an hundred and fifty and three: and for all there were so many, yet was not the net broken. Jesus saith unto them, Come and dine. And none of the disciples durst ask him, Who art thou? knowing that it was the Lord. Jesus then cometh, and taketh bread, and giveth them, and fish likewise. This is now the third time that Jesus shewed himself to his disciples, after that he was risen from the dead. So when they had dined, Jesus saith to Simon Peter, Simon, son of Jonas, lovest thou me more than these? He saith unto him, Yea, Lord; thou knowest that I love thee. He saith unto him, Feed my lambs. He saith to him again the second time, Simon, son of Jonas, lovest thou me? He saith unto him, Yea, Lord; thou knowest that I love thee. He saith unto him, Feed my sheep. He saith unto him the third time, Simon, son of Jonas, lovest thou me? Peter was grieved because he said unto him the third time, Lovest thou me? And he said unto him, Lord, thou knowest all things; thou knowest that I love thee. Jesus saith unto him, Feed my sheep. Verily, verily, I say unto thee, When thou wast young, thou girdest thyself, and walkedst whither thou wouldest:

but when thou shalt be old, thou shalt stretch forth thy hands, and another shall gird thee, and carry thee whither thou wouldest not. This spake he, signifying by what death he should glorify God. And when he had spoken this, he saith unto him, Follow me.

This story of Jesus's meeting with the disciples Thomas, Nathanael, and Simon Peter took place on the Sea of Galilee. It was shortly after the crucifixion of Jesus; and Peter was feeling very distraught about having scorned Jesus and not standing up for him as he had promised, for having denied him three times before the cock crowed as Jesus said he would.

Peter was a fisherman before Jesus had called him as a disciple. It was the only thing that Simon Peter knew. A tough, hard, and rugged man who was used to depending on himself for all his needs and provision; a strong man with strong convictions. He was devastated by what happened to Jesus and having denied him when he had the opportunity to declare him and be there for support.

He was afraid of what might happen to him, that he may be arrested too and suffer the same fate as Jesus, whatever that might be. When Jesus was arrested, there was chaos, and everybody went running for cover.

To be in that situation just after Jesus had told the disciples that He would be betrayed, put the spirit of fear on them and caused them to question everything. Their whole world had been shattered. Peter needed to be somewhere he could regroup and sort through things; he must have felt that being back out on the water would somehow help him to think, to rationalize things, and somehow let him get some understanding of all these events.

What did it all mean, what was it all for, where will he go from that point, how will he rebuild himself? All the time lost in following this man and seeing him crucified, how will he deal with all of it and what will he do now? How will he start over and where? All of his family, friends, and everybody in the community knew that he was a follower of Jesus. Was he thinking that, that was the biggest mistake of his life? How could he live with all the decisions he had made? Peter was an emotional mess and a completely lost soul, broken, and dejected, with all hope dashed.

The water was the place he knew best; he was hurt and in emotional pain, confused. He had lost his hope and felt he had let Jesus, the others, and himself down. Peter really did love Jesus; he really did believe that Jesus was the Messiah, but now what?

Go to the water. Do what you know to do, fish!

This is when Thomas and Nathanael said they would accompany him, so the three of them went to Peter's boat to fish. Perhaps the other two didn't trust Peter's state of mind at this time and didn't want him to be by himself, alone and on the water.

The thing is they didn't catch anything. The nets were empty until they heard a voice from the shore call out to them to try casting the net on the other side of the boat, and it was the voice of Jesus. When they did, the nets became full; and that was when they saw the fire that Jesus had prepared, that was when Jesus had beckoned to them to come and eat.

The thing is this, a similar scenario happened once before. When Jesus first met Simon Peter, it was because he had been fishing and caught nothing. Jesus told Peter and his companions to go back out and cast their nets again. Despite their doubt, they did as Jesus said, and the nets became so full that others had to join in to help pull the nets.

This is also where Jesus told them to follow Him, and He would make them fishers of men.

Maybe it was at this time Peter needed some reassurance because of the great devastation he had just been through. Maybe his spirit was so broken that it was the only way he could be restored, and Jesus knew this.

Jesus came to him maybe because he heard Peter's cry, maybe he felt his torment; either way, Jesus did have a personal encounter with Peter. Peter was restored and given a deeper level of faith. He was able to overcome his situation and go on to become one of the great leaders in the church. Millions of people heard of Jesus, and today, millions more because of Peter's obedience to Jesus's word "follow me."

It is through the obedience to the calling that you, yourself, are being restored. Restored from the existence you are living now, from the sorrows, the hurts, and the pains that life can scar you with. How can you expect a supernatural change without you doing something alongside of and with God? In other words, you must work on your own restoration daily. It is with your faith; remember, faith without works is dead. The works are prayer, fasting, studying the Word daily, bringing the gift God planted in you to the surface so that it may bring forth fruit that glorifies God and be a blessing to others. Learn all you can about your gift; this is your labor, so rejoice in it. Learn how to reap the harvest and how to make it available to others. Allow God to mold you and remake you; be willing to submit to him. Give yourself permission to forgive yourself for your shortcomings and start forgiving others. Then start on restoring yourself.

The Scriptures says work out first your own salvation.

> Philippians 2:12-15 (KJV)
>
> Wherefore, my beloved, as ye have always obeyed, not as in my presence only, but now much more in my absence, work out your own salvation with fear and trembling.
>
> For it is God which worketh in you both to will and to do of his good pleasure.
>
> Do all things without murmurings and disputings:
>
> That ye may be blameless and harmless, the sons of God, without rebuke, in the midst of a crooked and perverse nation, among whom ye shine as lights in the world

In that is where your restoration is found. It is through the work, the diligence, and above all, the obedience to follow Him.

The purpose to overcome the issues holding you back is to fulfill your purpose and being restored.

In recognizing these changes, you must ask, "Are you doing good, or are you doing God?"

Is the work you are doing fulfilling God's call and purpose in your life?

Does it glorify Him does it bring a blessing to others, and does it make provision for you?

Through prayer and fasting, God gives you an invitation; and in this invitation, He makes you a promise. In the promise is the planting of the seed, which is your gift. Once you have planted the seed, acknowledge it. Then comes the growing season in which your gift matures. As your gift matures, tests and temptations will come before you will be able to reap the harvest of your gift. These tests and temptations take on the form of ridicule from others who would keep you from being all God has called you to be. There will be doubters and naysayers, someone always trying to rain on your restoration parade. Recognize the obstacles and challenges that get in your way when they come; those negative things trying to stop you or block your blessings. Rejoice in them, knowing you are on the right track, and God has you covered.

Learn all you can about the gift God has planted in you; and in this is the harvest. It is in the labor that you find joy; rejoice in it, and do it as unto the Lord.

Even if you slip up and don't get it right the first or the seventh time, God forgives; and in his forgiveness, he will restore you.

All it takes is a personal encounter with Jesus.

Journal
The Tenth Hour
God Restores

Epilogue

You have had a personal encounter with Jesus; if not, go back, and do it again. Do it until you get your breakthrough.

Take it more seriously this time; be responsible for your own restoration.

God gives back in equal measure. God will take you as seriously as you take this work.

You are promised. You are gifted. You are called. You are anointed, and you are ordained by God to do his will.

You have a purpose in this life and that is to worship God. Through your worship, you will be fulfilled in the calling God has for you.

God will be glorified in it, others will be blessed by it; and by it, you shall receive your provision.

Start doing the things God has revealed to you. Let the fertile ground inside of you accept this seed as his purpose for you in your life and be renewed.

Let the Holy Spirit guide you. Let your heart be known for it is the heart of God, and God will order your steps. Bring in the harvest; and by your fruits, it will be known.

By your Faith, you shall Overcome and be Restored.

You are here F.O.R. a purpose.

I believe this book to be divinely inspired, given to me by the Holy Spirit to give to you for a purpose.

There are too many people that do not know why they are here and what it is that they are supposed to do with their lives. They don't know there is life after this life, life eternal, and they live unfulfilled lives. I believe God is reaching out to all of us in these dire days.

He desires for us to be blessed, healthy, and live a life of abundance if we but only trust in Him and put Him first in all we do. Jesus wants a personal encounter with each and every one of us.

We can be His light in this fallen and dark world, a shining example of His endless love and mercy and His forgiveness and compassion, which are given unto us by His grace so that we may receive the promise of Abraham, having joy unspeakable and life everlasting.

A New Day

This is the beginning of a new day
God has given me this day to use as I choose
I can waste it or make the best of it
But what I do with it is important
Because I am exchanging a day of my life for it
When tomorrow comes this day will be gone forever
Leaving in its place something I have traded for it
I want to prosper not suffer
I want a blessing not a curse; success and not failure
That I may not regret its price.

Psalm 118:24-29 (KJV)

This is the day which the Lord hath made; we will rejoice and be glad in it. Save now, I beseech thee, O Lord: O Lord, I beseech thee, send now prosperity. Blessed be he that cometh in the name of the Lord: we have blessed you out of the house of the Lord. God is the Lord, which hath shewed us light: bind the sacrifice with cords, even unto the horns of the altar. Thou art my God, and I will praise thee: thou art my God, I will exalt thee. O give thanks unto the Lord; for he is good: for his mercy endureth for ever.

⊖|LIVE

---

listen|imagine|view|experience

AUDIO BOOK DOWNLOAD INCLUDED WITH THIS BOOK!

In your hands you hold a complete digital entertainment package. In addition to the paper version, you receive a free download of the audio version of this book. Simply use the code listed below when visiting our website. Once downloaded to your computer, you can listen to the book through your computer's speakers, burn it to an audio CD or save the file to your portable music device (such as Apple's popular iPod) and listen on the go!

How to get your free audio book digital download:

1. Visit www.tatepublishing.com and click on the e|LIVE logo on the home page.
2. Enter the following coupon code:
   4a64-5fe7-178a-e2f5-bd0f-2380-e665-6432
3. Download the audio book from your e|LIVE digital locker and begin enjoying your new digital entertainment package today!